THE ART OF FRENCH
VEGETABLE GARDENING

THE ART OF FRENCH

BY LOUISA JONES   PHOTOGRAPHS BY

VEGETABLE GARDENING

GILLES LE SCANFF & JOËLLE CAROLINE MAYER

ARTISAN   NEW YORK

DESIGNER: JOEL AVIROM
PRODUCTION DIRECTOR: HOPE KOTURO

Published in 1995 by Artisan
A Division of Workman Publishing Company, Inc.
708 Broadway
New York, NY 10003

Library of Congress Cataloging-in-Publication Data
Jones, Louisa
The Art of French vegetable gardening / by Louisa Jones;
photographs by Gilles Le Scanff & Joëlle Caroline Mayer.
    Includes bibliographical references (p. 181) and index.
    ISBN 1-885183-09-7
1. Vegetable gardening—France.   2. Gardening—France.
3. Vegetable gardening—France—Pictorial works.
4. Gardening—France—Pictorial works.
5. Vegetable gardening.   6. Gardening.
I. Le Scanff, Gilles.   II. Mayer, Joëlle Caroline.   III. Title.
SB323.J66 1995
712'.6—dc20   95-9107

Printed in Italy
10 9 8 7 6 5 4 3 2 1
First Printing

For my oldest
and most unromantic
gardening crony

❧ CONTENTS

INTRODUCTION

As a Canadian expatriate who long lived in the Pacific northwestern United States before settling in southern France some twenty years ago, I have always been fascinated by how people relate to places. Gardening allows for a particularly rich dialogue between human beings and very local growing conditions—and traditions. To appreciate it means understanding "culture" in all senses. I began gardening in France in 1975, and soon realized that contemporary French gardeners look very much to England for their inspiration today—sometimes at the cost of neglecting their own heritage.

And how do English garden experts regard the French? Anne Scott James explains in her *Gardening Letters to My Daughter* that "French gardening is either brilliant or catastrophic." The best examples, she claims, are the grand ones, such as Versailles, Vaux-le-Vicomte, and Fontainebleau—"nothing there for the little man to copy." But then almost as an afterthought, she adds, "The other glory of French gardening is the vegetable section, so perfectly cultivated that pretentious English gardeners now call their vegetable patches potagers, justified by a bit of box edging and a couple of espalier apples or pear."

French vegetable gardens have indeed furnished a model for most of the western world, raising the simple production of family food to perfection for both the palate and the eye. And there is much there "for the little man to copy." French potagers come in all shapes and sizes, and are cultivated by people of all means and backgrounds. Every French château has its walled, rectangular kitchen garden, often of great beauty. Saint-Jean-de-Beauregard south of Paris and the Château of Miromesnil in Normandy count among the most appealing, maintained today in a family style. At the same time, anonymous and unsung, but visible along every winding rural road, are the delightful plots of farmers and country people tucked into the most surprising and irregular spaces, where not a foot of soil is wasted. Far less well known still are the allotment gardens—strips of land given over to the intense production of vegetables and cultivated by gardeners living in town, meeting there after work or on weekends to swap seeds, cuttings, and advice. Some of these sites have existed for over a hundred years; others have disappeared as many city gardeners acquired their own homes and put the potager in their own backyard. But wherever it takes place—city, suburb, country, or château—French vegetable gardening continues to be a national passion. In 1994, the French government survey office estimated that 23 percent of all fruit and vegetables consumed in France are home-grown. And each section of this country in which regional styles are so richly marked

❧ Since Medieval times, French vegetables have been grown together with fruit, flowers, and aromatics, combined in different ways for both pleasure and profit.

and varied has its own type of potager, deeply rooted, so to speak, in the rural architecture and landscapes of the local *terroir*.

Today, the best French garden architects are creating sophisticated designer potagers. And the fashion for decorative vegetable gardening, so strong now in England and America, looks once more to France for inspiration. The intricate vegetable parterres of the Château de Villandry, a modern creation based on Renaissance models, have been imitated and adapted by many admirers, none more influential than Rosemary Verey at Barnsley House in England. But others prefer another French model: the *jardin de curé,* interpreted in modern times as a homey, intimate and even half-wild style of gardening which bows to nature's whimsy rather than imposing strong design and control. This style of potager became very popular in the sixties and seventies, when organic gardening swept France as elsewhere.

Today, France offers an unparalleled range of potagers, from medicinal gardens restored around medieval abbeys to collections of rare exotica grown by plant specialists and . . . great chefs. However varied in its inspiration throughout the centuries, the art of French vegetable gardening has always meant growing fruit, herbs, and flowers as well as vegetables. And, however fashionable, the French potager continues to signify for many of its adepts a very deep communion with the earth, a mutually beneficial partnership on a human scale, a hopeful model of symbiosis between humankind and nature, the very antithesis of voracious agribusiness. "A garden," says American writer Michael Pollan in his wise book *Second Nature*, "will move us to the extent it engages the imagination as well as the senses." Few types of gardening have done this for such a wide range of people over as many centuries as has the French vegetable garden.

Louisa Jones
Ardèche, 1995

ACKNOWLEDGMENTS

ACKNOWLEDGMENTS AND THANKS: to the many garden owners who so graciously answered questions and swapped seeds, advice, and cuttings; to Leslie Stoker for her constant thoughtfulness and good humor; to Joëlle Caroline Mayer and Gilles Le Scanff for their enthusiastic, talented, and conscientious efforts in illustrating this book; to Georges Lévêque for his usual generosity; to François Chaslin and Annie François for encouragement and precious resources; to Philippe Ferret for sharing the benefits of his rich experience; to Charlotte Lindgren for her valuable insights; to Anne Willan and Marc Cherniavsky for allowing liberal use of their wonderful library; to Lydia Christofides, for faithfully sending seeds year after year; to Simone Chazalet, who has been the guardian angel for my potager since its beginnings; to my *belle-famille* for years of patience and encouragement.

–LOUISA JONES

We wish to express our most sincere gratitude to all the garden owners and gardeners who, by opening the gate of their vegetable gardens to us, made the photographs of this book possible.
-experimental garden, from *L'Ami des Jardin et de la Maison*
-Jean Bardet's old-fashioned, romantic garden in Tours
-Pierre Bourgois' conservatory in Charente-Maritime
-vegetable garden north of Chantilly, dating from about 1850
-conservatory of gardens, Chaumont-sur-Loire
-Jean-Paul Collaert's garden
-the Marquise de Bagneux's "La Coquetterie" (garden) in Limesy, Seine-Maritime
-Ambassador and Madame Robert Gillet's gardens at Château de Galleville
-Bruno Goris' vegetable garden in Goudon
-garden in the Hurepoix
-Mr. and Mrs. Lafourcade's garden near Saint-Rémy-de-Provence
-vegetable garden in the Massif Central
-"jardin de la Massionière" at St. Christophe-en-Champagne
-vegetable garden of Marc Meneau, chef-restaurateur at L'Espérance in Yonne
-Château de Miromesnil
-vegetable garden in the mountains of Lyon
-vegetable garden in Orne
-garden of a newly retired man on the Arvert Peninsula
-ethnobotanical garden in Salagon
-vegetable garden at the Château de St. Jean-de-Beauregard in Essone
-Château de St. Paterne at the gates of Alençon
-Château and garden of Villandry, near Tours
-parish priest's garden at "Wy Dit Joli Village" in Val d'Oise

Our thanks also go to Yves Pechon for his friendly assistance and to all garden owners who chose to remain anonymous.

–GILLES LE SCANFF and JOËLLE CAROLINE MAYER

STYLE

The world of French potagers has amazing diversity—indeed, some 60 percent of the private gardens in France contain vegetables. Two opposing trends predominate: the strictly formal approach on the one hand, and the romantically exuberant on the other. Neat rows and squares recall the geometric parterres of old château gardens and even older abbey and monastery plots. But another tradition welcomes a profusion of flowers, vegetables, and aromatics in haphazard array. This type of garden is often called the *jardin de curé,* a kind of country or cottage garden. Each of these two major styles, the formal and the romantic, has its history, which has in turn determined its major characteristics.

FORMAL VEGETABLE GARDENING

European gardens, it has been said, began in the monastery: an intimate space whose high enclosure protected the plants that provided food, clothing, medicine, and beauty for the altar. Nature lay at large outside the walls, and gardening meant reclaiming nature by human arts and skills. Walls marked the transition, in the telling phrase of one seventeenth-century garden writer, between "the neat and the rude." Its ancestor was, after all, the paradise garden, the oasis in the desert. The wilderness that lay beyond the monastery walls was like the unredeemed soul in need of spiritual initiation—nurturing, pruning, and overall gentle cultivation. In the thirteenth-century allegorical tale the *Romance of the Rose* the vices appear as brambles and nettles that hinder the hero's progress toward the rose in the heart of the garden.

Cloister gardens inevitably used formal design. In a period when all spatial detail carried heavy symbolism, the cloister was divided into four parts by two intersecting paths that met in the center at a fountain. Thus the shape of a cross was immediately visible, spread out around water, the source of life. When the famous ornamental potager at the Château de Villandry near Tours was laid out early in this century, its conception coincided with the owner's conversion to Catholicism. As a result its design once again repeats the form of the cross in infinite variation.

❧ *Above:* **The complex formal patterns of the famous potager at the Château de Villandry, near Tours, have inspired ornamental vegetable gardens all over the world. Modeled on Renaissance parterres, they were created by Joachim Carvallo as of 1906.**
❧ *Opposite:* **Traditional row plantings may lose their geometries by midsummer as here, where lush growth creates a spreading sea of beans.**

🌿 *ABOVE:* **Formal vegetable gardeners pride themselves on neat rows alternating with well-tended strips of bare earth. Flowers are usually grown by themselves on the edge of the potager.**
🌿 *OPPOSITE:* **The potager at Miromesnil in Normandy is fast becoming known as a particularly beautiful château garden. Its high walls shelter a rich array of everything from asparagus to rambling roses. As always, there is a greenhouse to prolong the seasons, both spring and fall.**

Many French gardeners today still enjoy a monastic sense of contrast between the work of mankind, clearly defined as such, and nature's unredeemed or simply untamed vast expanses. Writer Pierre Gascar grows flowers and vegetables on sunny terraces, beyond which stretch the forests of the Jura—uninterrupted, he claims, as far as Transylvania. The garden's walls and domesticated plants offer to him, instead of the limitless liberty of the forest, another freedom, that of ever-deepening possession. Here, he says, he can travel without moving from the spot, gradually entering into the secrets of earthly, and earthy, dimensions. His densely planted patch also offers a path to spiritual initiation, a vertical dimension not unlike that of its ancestor, the cloister garden, though the latter looked up toward heaven and Gascar bends earthward. His garden and the adjacent forest present a microcosm of the world's possibilities. Many Americans, responding to a different cultural heritage, might prefer the wilderness of the nearby forest.

In the classic medieval garden, one part was devoted to medicinal herbs, another to vegetables, a third to fruit, and a fourth to growing flowers that would decorate the altar of the adjoining church. Thus the decorative vegetable garden is not a modern conceit, but an ongoing, centuries-old tradition that was interrupted—quite briefly in the great scheme of things—by the rigid separation of ornamental and utilitarian gardens that occurred in France as of the Renaissance and in England in the early Jacobean period.

When this break took place, the kitchen garden was hidden away from the pleasure garden, which in turn became more and more strongly visual in its attractions. If flowers had previously been grown for many different reasons—to provide dyes or medicines or scented petals to be used as carpets or potpourri—they now appealed above all to the eye. In France flowers counted less and less in the theatrical design of grand vistas, with carefully planned vantage and focal points which came to dominate gardening. Thus evolved the French château park, of which the most famous example is Versailles.

Grandeur, spectacle, show, disdain for the humble vegetable and the merely utilitarian? Anne Scott-James, in her delightful history of the pleasure garden, comments that André Le Nôtre, Louis XIV's head gardener, was so little interested in plants for their own sake that he could hardly be imagined talking to his trees.

Even today the name of Le Nôtre evokes for gardeners vast formal parterres laid out around a strong central axis, designs in which mankind's mastery of nature is arrogantly reaffirmed. But like most stereotypes, this one oversimplifies. Le Nôtre was not above choosing, for his coat of arms, a spade surrounded by slugs and topped with cabbage leaves.

Versailles had a famous potager, conceived and planted not by Le Nôtre but by France's most famous vegetable gardener: Jean de La Quintinye. It, too, illustrated man's domination over nature: Because the king wanted to be able to look down upon the patterned plots of vegetables from the terrace above, he insisted that they be planted in marshy land that La Quintinye himself described as "the sort that no one would ever want." It took cartloads and cartloads of horse manure and imported soil simply to prepare the terrain. Today the Potager de Versailles is among the best known in the country.

Some of the most handsome vegetable gardens in France still belong to other seventeenth- and eighteenth-century châteaux, however, set apart from the formal parterres and surrounded by high walls. Many are open to the public, and indeed, in recent times, there has been a fashion among château owners, themselves perhaps bored with too many box parterres, to restore their vegetable gardens. Those at Saint-Jean-de-Beauregard near Paris and at Miromesnil in Normandy are among the best known and most beautiful.

There exists another strong tradition of formal vegetable gardening in France: the peasant garden. Rural families today still arrange their vegetables with the strict rigor of well-grown rows. Working-class gardens, those that developed at the time of the Industrial Revolution when factory housing often included small vegetable plots for each family, also proudly sported even, regular rows, carefully aligned and tended. A recent issue of the railroad employees' gardening magazine, *Le Cheminot,* praises "vegetables laid out in straight rows, well-dug soil and clean paths" as "the ideal of any good gardener."

Writer Jean-Jacques Salgon remembers his childhood in a small town in the Ardèche, where his father was a grade-school teacher, the kind of *instituteur* for whom it was a vocation to bring education to remote rural areas. He found time for a potager, however, like his peasant neighbors. Salgon recalls the importance of its classical symmetry:

> The geometry of the vegetable garden, very early, educated my eye.
>
> From earth upturned from the earliest days of spring, like a blackboard that has been erased, soon sprang, under my father's Cartesian footsteps, a whole network of paths and passages that formed a complex and multi-branched topography outlining the territory allotted to each vegetable, and the natural borders offered to the garden's future inhabitants. Thus emerged, as from the pen of a mapmaker, the emirate of the asparagus, the radish square, the republic of carrots and lettuce, the marquisat of sorrel and the principalities of celery and parsley.
>
> These countries that at first existed only as pure forms already belied, as in Zen gardens, the pure contours of knowledge, the architecture of ancient wisdom.

Might it be said that such rigorous formal organization represents the spirit of Versailles transferred to the backyard country plot? Comparable to the constant control required to maintain fruit trees in complex espaliered forms and cordons—the human hand laid hard and fast on natural expansion?

There may well be another explanation. Another writer and famous gardener, Colette, records her own experiments in this domain. Like many leisured enthusiasts, growing vegetables for pleasure and not to supplement a meager family budget, she fell out with her peasant gar-

❧ Contemporary designers invent new geometries. Philippe Ferret created this elegant potager as a model for readers of the popular French gardening magazine, *L'Ami des jardins.* He has a fine sense of proportion and volume.

🌿 *ABOVE:* **At Miromesnil, formal floral borders along the high walls do not preclude blooms among the vegetables.**
🌿 *OVERLEAF LEFT:* **Dahlias brighten up Swiss chard in this romantic blend around a small forest of wooden stakes.**
🌿 *OVERLEAF RIGHT:* **Basil and chives, single-flowered hollyhocks and lettuce, artichokes and dahlias, at different stages of growth, happily share the terrain.**

dener over just this question. When she first settled in Saint-Tropez in 1927, she was determined to have an exuberant intermingling of vegetables and flowers, vistas of tumbling roses. No geometry, she insisted, no even rows! The "spirit of the place," an old "horticultural gardener" whose hair is as curly as cypress foliage, nods but resists. The plantings he proposes look, she exclaims, like a barbecue grill. But after the first season, she comes to understand that his motives are not simply the rigid adherence to tradition, nor a desire to impose proud human domination on natural haphazardness. Nature is far too immense and unpredictable to submit to such puny efforts, especially in the Mediterranean world. Geometry, on this soil that has known millennia of cultivation, simply means attempting, year after year, to come to terms with nature in the most tentative manner. The peasants grow their hedges and set up their reed curtains to keep out the wind, notes Colette, and behind these walls they set out gardens that are "blooming but fearful." The ancient wisdom is not abstract and theoretical, but results from generations of experience. She gives in, and regards her early fancies as "serious lapses in taste."

ROMANTIC VEGETABLE GARDENING

Other gardeners have persisted, however, with Colette's dream of untamed intermingling of colors, smells, sounds, and tastes. This romantic model continues to appeal to many French vegetable gardeners, though perhaps it is true that it remains a luxury not permitted to those gardeners for whom it is essential to produce the maximum amount of food with the least effort and expense. Orderly vegetable gardening was a necessity for the poor and not only an avatar of the French classical spirit.

Sometimes (in good romantic tradition) the difference lies only in the eye of the beholder. If Jean-Jacques Salgon admired his father's formal geometries, he also pictured him constantly gardening among his roses, peonies, cherry trees, carrots, and green beans in a pale light, by the fountain—the very picture of a sentimental childhood. Impressionist painters often transposed the geometries of market gardens around Paris into spots of color and light overflowing the strictly geometrical limits of the gardener's original plantations. And even Henry James was moved to lyricism in 1882 when he peered over the fourteenth-century ramparts of the city of Poitiers at a patchwork hillside "peopled with cabbages and carrots . . . the charming little vegetable-gardens with which the base of the hill appears exclusively to be garnished." However strictly their owners maintain order, taken together these plots form a deliciously romantic prospect.

Nonetheless, these two tendencies usually stand as two opposing styles. When Pierre Gascar wrote a lyric homage to his vegetable garden in his book *Un Jardin de curé,* he began by trying to distinguish the classical style from the romantic, deciding that the first insists on forms imposed by the human hand, the second aims at looking spontaneous, hiding human efforts as much as possible. In the romantic potager, straight lines are rare, and if plants are grown in rows, they are so intermingled with companion plantings or chance contributions that the lines are hard to distinguish. Secondly, he explains, such gardens do indeed welcome offerings brought by the wind, or by birds, or simply by neighboring gardeners. Their owners do not view weeds as dangerous interlopers liable to disturb well-established order, but rather as unexpected bounty. Or, as Ralph Waldo Emerson put it: "What is a weed? A plant whose virtues have not yet been discovered!" And if, in order to produce any vegetables at all, romantic owners are nonetheless obliged to remove a good number of these gifts, enough remain to give an overall impression of cheerful disorder.

In France, classical tradition has for centuries encouraged the rational separation of logical categories—comedy does not mix with tragedy in the theater, for example. Romantic potagers are more Shakespearean—they recklessly mingle flowers and vegetables, fruit and herbs, not in separate beds but all together. Sometimes this happens by chance, sometimes according to various theories of beneficial associations. Plants that are introduced by hopeful gardeners are

allowed to self-sow where they will. The intense blue of borage, the deep wine-red of rhubarb chard, small lettuces, and corn salad thus pop up all over the garden.

Gascar enjoys such potagers for their unexpected gifts and also for the surprises of their design: "Clumps of shrubbery block the perspectives and turn paths into labyrinths, leading to hidden corners, creating the feeling of a peaceful world apart." Meandering through it, he feels, the gardener enjoys the rich solitude of a private Eden.

The two authors of a very practical but witty gardening guide called *The Lazy Man's Beautiful Garden,* Patricia Beuchert and Jean-Paul Collaert, also oppose strict order to romantic disarray in the art of French vegetable gardening. Which approach produces the most beautiful potager? they ask. It is true that adepts of the second mode tend to be *bricoleurs,* handymen who put together bits and pieces with whatever they have at hand: Old inner tubes or fertilizer sacks appear in odd corners, with wooden stakes, or mirrors. In this romantic mode, a garden shelter may grow up out of old crates tied together with string. But after all, they point out, the formal gardener may well put up a neat shed in bright green plastic, which is even uglier. The romantic gardener will have huge, starry quilts of sweet william in odd corners. His shed will be engulfed in cosmos, dahlias, and morning glories. There will be a trellis with wisteria or a vine providing shade over a table where the owner sits drinking pastis with two or three cohorts.

They agree that the romantic potager is a world unto itself, a small, separate kingdom—with the emphasis on "small." For even where the actual plot can be considered large, the profusion of plants in a romantic potager gives a feeling of enclosure, of microcosm, of reduced scale. Perhaps this is true also because plant texture and perfume count so much more than proportion and perspective in this case.

The romantic French garden has its own prestigious heritage. Such a scene was imagined by none other than Jean-Jacques Rousseau in his influential novel, *Julie, ou la nouvelle Héloïse,* first published in 1761. Rousseau's idealized heroine creates a beautiful woodland garden, a "disguised orchard" brimming over with flowers and birdsong, that strikes the imagination as forcefully as the senses. The illusion of wilderness is so complete, says the writer, that he feels like the first mortal ever to penetrate it. He notes that all the plants chosen are varieties that grow naturally in this landscape, nothing exotic. But herbs such as thyme, balm, and marjoram spread under rosebushes, raspberries, and gooseberries, while lilac, hazelnut trees, and broom intermingle, all of it "disposed without any order or symmetry." This profusion adds beauty but at the same time makes the ground look as if overgrown with weeds. The paths are irregular and "serpentine," "bordered by these flowery thickets" and garlanded with many fragrant climbers. And always, throughout, there is birdsong.

Better known today, but certainly influenced by Rousseau, is the model of the *jardin de curé,* or country priest's garden. In rural villages, the *curé* would often have a small house with a garden near the church, to help him eke out a meager living. Here too would be grown flowers to decorate the church, and their haphazard intermingling came not so much from the bounties of nature as from those of the parishioners, who would bring cuttings, seeds, and plants whenever their own gardens were overflowing. The *jardin de curé* is often proposed as the French equivalent of the cottage garden; and certainly its name evokes for readers today a similarly nostalgic vision of a small garden packed with colorful plants grown for use as well as for visual pleasure. The plants that found their way there came as if seeking asylum. As a result, these plots also preserved old country varieties, unnamed and otherwise lost, as did the English cottage gardens. Pierre Gascar notes that the treasures of the *jardin de curé* came by twos and threes at best, and were never planted in large swaths. He calls these gardens veritable Noah's arks of vegetable and flower varieties. For him, this style also implies a devotion to the fruits of the earth, a kind of homage that is a form of worship.

❧ In this contemporary garden near Paris, bright blooms, espaliered fruit, aromatics, and vegetables intermingle near the village church. In old-fashioned curates' gardens, flowers were used to decorate the altar and aromatics for medicinal purposes.

The *jardin de curé* differs from the English cottage garden, however, in that the latter is visible from the street, while the priest's plot was hidden behind high walls, a private and intimate space open to the sky, like the cloister garden before it. Often it also had the two crossed paths around a fountain.

The grand historical gardens associated with the late-eighteenth- and early-nineteenth-century movement properly called Romanticism might seem the antithesis of the *jardin de curé,* for they were composed of vast landscapes, themselves modeled after the Italian scenes painted by Nicolas Poussin and Claude Lorrain, in turn reinterpreted by the great English landscapers, William Kent and "Capability" Brown. These were not plantsmen's gardens even for flowers, much less vegetables. And they were predominantly, almost militantly, visual, concerned with vast perspectives, whereas the potager tradition has always appealed to all the senses at once. But the romantic potager style may nonetheless be associated with these prestigious precedents, in spite of its small scale and dense plantings, because of its shared refusal of the straight line and its similar desire to incorporate nature's chance bounties. And just as the historical Romantic gardening tradition often went to great lengths to prepare most carefully an illusion of spontaneity, just as Rousseau's artfully planted orchard seemed untouched by human hand, so the seeming disarray of the romantic style in vegetable gardening often requires more work than do conventionally ordered rows. Where everything is irregular, upkeep must often be done by hand, without machinery. Romantic gardens with a capital "R" and their modest vegetable counterpart are all gardens that look "natural" but require a lot of effort.

Unless, of course, the owner really does just let everything run wild. An English gardener, Lady Fortescue, describes in her book *Perfume from Provence* her attempts to garden on the Riviera in the 1950's. Her own hired hand, Hilaire, is a hardworking soul from the nearby village, familiar with all the local weather patterns, watering practices, and so on. He gets very angry with their neighbor, a certain Pierre, who keeps bees and lets all his good terraced hillside run to wildflowers. Excellent vegetables could be grown there, complains Hilaire, and Pierre is a lazy good-for-nothing. Lady Fortescue much prefers Pierre's wildflowers to the garish bedding plants with which Hilaire insists on filling up her flower beds (he finds her taste for pastels "triste"). But she admits that no one is better with the vegetable garden than orderly, hardworking Hilaire. She does not say if Pierre manages, nonetheless, to produce vegetables or if he lives on nectar and ambrosia alone . . .

Sometimes potagers begin the season in strict formality and end up romantic by September! And sometimes, of course, the wild, romantic style is simply a fallback position for the tired gardener, when weeds get the upper hand. American writer Gertrude Stein and her companion Alice B. Toklas kept beautiful gardens for years in the Bugey region southeast of Lyons. Their intentions were classical: Gertrude looked after the flowers and Alice, whose interest was the

✣ **At the Château de Saint-Paterne near Alençon, local Laotian families have created an exuberant, organically grown potager in the romantic style.**

table, tended two vast vegetable gardens, which she made not only productive but very ornamental. There were moments, however, when the effort of maintenance became overwhelming. When Stein asked Toklas what she saw when she closed her eyes, the latter answered "Weeds!" At harvest time, though, Toklas professed lavish and romantic admiration for their mounds of squash and beans and other produce, which she insisted on having shipped to Paris for use during the winter, regardless of Stein's protestations that this would be costly and impractical. Many contemporary gardeners will sympathize with her pride.

Today, French romantics often belong to the ecological persuasion. The magazine *Les Quatre saisons,* bible of French organic gardeners, is full of ideas for cheap structures to be made of recycled materials, companion plantings, gardening by the moon, and so on. The spaces between vegetables are filled with green manures, either growing strong or cut and piled deep as mulch, or with flowers and herbs chosen for specific beneficial properties. The result is often a garden design submerged by the density and variety of the plantings.

There is much nostalgia in this vision—and that in itself, of course, is romantic. Today's most successful romantic potagers do tend to create the sense of a lost Eden, a mini-paradise that is fragile and eternal all at once. These gardens are very difficult to photograph, much easier to sketch or describe. Their appeal is ineffable, one of charm rather than of objectively calculated proportion or design. In some respects, romantic potagers are the most extreme case of the French decorative vegetable garden because they imply owners willing, more than most, to risk hard productivity for an ideal, self-contained world of beauty. They imply also that the owner has time, or will take time, not only to be a performer on this stage, or the stagehand behind the scenes, but also the spectator—whether meandering appreciatively through the garden observing birds, insects, and individual plants as they grow, or drinking pastis under the trellis with friends. Indeed, in the romantic style, the garden owner is often also the person working the land, with or without help, whereas in the formal style, there is often a professional gardener distinct from the owner.

Decorative vegetable gardening today, in France as elsewhere, often requires this double vision of rigorous practical organization on the one hand, the view from inside, so to speak, and, on the other, the distanced spectator's ability to see the poetry of the show as it evolves through the seasons. Each gardener must decide on the balance he or she wants between productivity and romance, order and charm, and each will of course have different ideas as to what constitutes "tasteful" presentation, in all senses of the word. But in a country where, for centuries, gardeners from all classes of society have produced potagers that still command attention for their beauty, much can be learned from both past and present practice.

❧ OUTLINES

Vegetable gardens in France as elsewhere have basic practical requirements. These were quite efficiently summarized by Louis XIV's gardener, La Quintinye, already in the seventeenth century: The ground chosen must "be good whatever the Colour be"; the situation must be favorable; there must be "a good convenience to water"; the garden should be set "upon a small rising"; it should be "of an agreeable Figure . . . enclos'd with reasonably high walls," and the access should be "easy and convenient."

THE SITE

The point of this expert's advice is to protect vegetables from all the many dangers of weather and topography. La Quintinye recommends a favorable situation near the bottom of slopes—not on marshy valley land (such as he himself had to cope with at Versailles), not in frost pockets, but low enough to catch water and soil that will be washed down from higher ground. Walls were intended to protect vegetables from prevailing winds, and to extend the growing season by creating favorable microclimates.

If several sites can meet these practical requirements, La Quintinye then wonders where the potager should be located with respect to the house (usually a château in his time): If there is enough space, he says, the area nearest should be kept for flowers and parterres and the potager should be on the best ground beyond that is still readily accessible. But for "such as can have but one Garden, it will be far better to employ it in Fruits and Legumes than in Box and Grass."

Throughout the ensuing centuries, French potagers tended to be set apart in an enclosure of their own. Usually such sites have great appeal: Brick or stone walls covered with mosses and lichens protect them; permanent structures like *orangeries* shelter their pots and tools; weathered old trees nearby provide shade and link the garden to the buildings and the surrounding landscape.

In recently created vegetable gardens, even those intended above all to be ornamental, some French owners still set the potager

❧ *ABOVE:* **At Miromesnil, outlines are carefully maintained in the midst of profusion. Squash plants are grown between low edgers to keep them off the path— although** *Salvia horminum* **has sown itelf prettily among the big saucer leaves.**
❧ *OPPOSITE:* **At the nearby Château de Galleville, grass paths, formal hedges, and dwarf box edging make outlines clear and elegant but require high maintenance.**

apart from the house and the rest of the garden and keep it walled or partially enclosed. At the domain of La Massonnière near Le Mans, formal parterres, intricate topiary, mixed borders, and a wild garden surround the house, while the potager lies on a long strip of land, behind a high wall, at the bottom of the garden. In such cases, the vegetable garden remains a world of its own, partly because its upkeep requires different treatment from other styles of gardening, partly because the potager has a special, intimate atmosphere that even professional designers like to cultivate, so to speak. Other owners take the opposite approach, however. They judge that new potagers provide pleasure for the eye as well as the palate and therefore need not be kept out of sight like some merely utilitarian appendage. In this case, the garden will perhaps even be framed by the window of the house nearby, a cherished picture to be enjoyed for its constantly changing composition.

In the siting of a new decorative potager, it is important to keep in mind not only the practical constraints of weather and topography but the garden itinerary as a whole. When will the vegetable garden be seen by visitors, by the owners, before and after what other sorts of plantings? Above all, from what vantage point or points will it be visible? These questions will determine to what extent it will be walled and secret, or dramatically displayed. It may be admired from the entrance gate only, or from a house window or terrace; its entire pattern may be seen from above laid out as a glorious panorama; or perhaps one may come upon it suddenly as upon hidden treasure.

Few contemporary gardeners can afford or would even desire the major transformations of the natural landscape imposed by the Sun King at Versailles. But many contemporaries share his desire to treat their potagers as a kind of living, multicolored tapestry. Garden designers often speak of composing

❧ Many formal French potagers use low fruit cordons along the main paths of the potager, kept separate from the rest of the garden by high walls or hedging. This is La Massonnière, near Le Mans, southwest of Paris.

pictures, and this can well apply to vegetable gardens as well as to mixed borders. But it is then crucial to consider where the viewer sits or stands with respect to the picture composed.

THE SHAPE

Not only the siting but the entire layout of the vegetable plot will be affected by the vantage point. The shape and proportions of the picture as seen from one place or another will inevitably have tremendous importance for its beauty. Few gardeners begin with the poet's "white page"—a unmarked landscape to design at will. Most, however, can modify somewhat the dimensions of their chosen site, making the cultivated plot longer or broader, linking it to surrounding trees, hills, buildings to create the most pleasing proportions for the eye. Where dimensions must remain invariable, visual tricks can be played that make space look longer or shorter than it is. Bright red roses at the far end, for example, or a tall hedge, will bring the horizon line closer.

Here again, La Quintinye offers interesting advice, for his concern is as much for the pleasing proportion of the garden as its productivity. "The best figure for a Fruit or Kitchen Garden and most convenient for Culture is a beautiful Square [rectangle in today's language] of straight angles, being once and a half if not twice as long as 'tis broad." The entrance, he says, should be placed in the short side of the design and face a broad path extending the whole length of the potager, and thus "appear stately." If this creates subsections that are too long and narrow, they should be divided by smaller paths perpendicular to the main one. And so they usually are. Sometimes, indeed, where hedging is used inside the vegetable garden, it creates a series of green rooms, each with a different character. Thus again at the formal La Massonnière, and in the romantic Riviera potager of Bruno Goris, a professional gardener and consultant fast becoming known north of Nice. Here a series of hedged compartments enclose a central axis, although this remains a small, family garden. La Quintinye, however, belonging to the period of great formal parterres, intended the design to be entirely visible from the entrance.

Practical questions play an important part in determining shape, particularly the way the garden will be watered. If one or more elevated sprinklers will be used, each will probably cover a large rectangle. The garden's design may be adjusted so that no corners will be left high and dry, unless, of course, the gardener wishes to reserve a section for vegetables that do not appreciate water on their leaves, like tomatoes and cucurbits. If one part is to be supplied with a drip system, piping should be buried whenever possible even before paths are laid out.

Château vegetable gardens, like those of monastery cloisters, their ancestors, spread out in a square or rectangle around a central basin. The magic central circle of water has strong appeal even today, and occurs over and over

❧ French châteaux potagers are traditionally hidden away from the main garden and usually occupy one hectare of land (2.2 acres). The weathered brick paths at Miromesnil add warmth as well as clarity.

again: at La Massonnière, surrounded by lavender, at the Château de Villandry with its immense vegetable parterre surrounded by arbors, and in many others. Such designs are very beautiful, but a hidden pump and connections will be necessary for any practical use of this water in a contemporary garden, where hand-watering rarely suffices, even when anyone can be found to do it. Often today such basins remain purely decorative, and water for the vegetables comes from somewhere else entirely: At the Château de Saint-Jean-de-Beauregard, where some 10,000 square meters of vegetable garden lie around an elegant basin, the beds are watered from a lake just outside the walled potager. Hidden pipes empty the precious supply into cast-iron drums set discreetly here and there in the borders.

However regular the layout, the composition of a vegetable garden is always changing. Even in the extravagantly theatrical potagers of grand châteaux such as Versailles and Villandry, plantings must evolve from season to season. It is hard to

❧ *RIGHT:* At Saint-Jean-de-Beauregard near Paris, cast-iron drums discreetly set among the vegetation are filled from a lake outside the potager walls. This allows the water to warm up before being used to irrigate the vegetables.
❧ *OPPOSITE:* The broad basin that lies right in the heart of the potager at Saint-Jean-de-Beauregard is edged with purple and white strips of *Salvia farinacea* 'Victoria'. It is now purely decorative, since water is piped in from outside.

imagine a flower border dug up and redesigned yearly or even biannually, yet such feats of virtuosity are commonly performed by vegetable gardeners of every persuasion. In this type of gardening, where impermanence is not only a danger but a continuing challenge, strong, well-defined outlines and carefully balanced proportions count more than ever. The placing of permanent features—paths, constructions, trees, and so on—plays an essential role in establishing outlines. They must be chosen carefully for maximum practicality combined with greatest beauty.

ROWS, BEDS, AND PATHS

Once the site has been selected and its general shape established, the essential question arises: How to arrange the vegetables? Old-fashioned producers swear by strictly ordered rows and paths, both of variable width according to the owner's philosophy and the crops grown. Traditional French potagers are laid out with a line and stakes, in the formal style, with bare earth visible between the rows. Even some organic gardeners today maintain this heritage and follow the model of German writer Gertrud Franck. She recommends row plantings that are equally orderly and impeccably measured—but there is no bare earth. Assuming a large, rectangular plot, Franck plants the large, season-long crops like tomatoes or cucumbers at roughly 6-foot intervals, crops that mature in half a season 3 feet apart, and those that can be replaced several times at 18-inch intervals. And between each of these several types of row are lines of spinach in spring, as a sort of green manure to be cut and left on the spot, covered during the season by other garden debris and straw. Bare earth would be a sign of failure in such a garden, where a mixture of green manures and discreet sheet composting between rows keeps soil moist and fed. The following year, everything simply moves over 10 inches so that last year's composted paths become this year's rows. Franck's method succeeds best in climate zones with sufficient summer rain, in which case

🌿 *ABOVE & OPPOSITE:* **Garden designer Pascal Cribier created a famous checkerboard garden for the manor house at Limésy, in Normandy. Herbs, shrubs, perennials, and vegetables all contribute to the parterre. Plants are mostly grown singly, in separate blocks and cubes, outlined with paving blocks and separated by broad gravel-lined paths. Along one side, hornbeams have been trained into unusual shapes to provide support for tomatoes.**

the results can have much charm and appeal. One French devotee has compared this style to a musical partition.

Many French vegetable gardeners prefer beds to rows, their size and outline often determined by the kind of equipment used to cultivate the soil. Landscape designer Pascal Cribier, one of those restoring the Tuileries Gardens in the heart of Paris, has created a stunning parterre at Limésy, in Normandy, with a series of thirty-six squares along a vast esplanade that is enclosed at one end by a manor house and at the other by stables. Each bed is a bit more than 6 feet along each side. The composition mixes shrubs, perennials, vegetables, and herbs in such a way that there is a permanent basis for year-round beauty, but a kind of checkerboard movement among the annuals and vegetables that can be varied ad infinitum. It is a relatively low-maintenance garden in which each square grows only one type of plant in a solid block. Thyme, mint, basil, oregano, chives thus alternate with leeks, multicolored lettuces, garlic, potatoes, and red and green cabbages. Elsewhere are artichoke fountains, low-clipped spruce in a flat, evergreen cube, brilliant daylilies, sedum 'Autumn Joy', zinnias and chrysanthemums, irises, densely pruned forsythia, and dwarf willows. The effect is beautiful, but obviously decor here takes precedence over productivity.

A well-known French garden writer, Michèle Lamontagne, suggests a fresh and ornamental approach using squares the same size as Cribier's (6 feet a side), but planting them as double triangles separated by a strong diagonal—red lettuce, or a low-growing herb. At Vézelay, chef Marc Meneau, one of the stars of the French gastronomic world, chose a long rectangular site enclosed by a wall and hedging, in which he also uses square beds, in two parallel rows separated by a central path. Each pair of beds facing each other across the central path has the same plantings. Each square bed is moreover divided into four triangles, raised in the center around some vertical accent. Thus, for example, around a tall spray of angelica there will be a triangle of squash plants, another of bush thyme (a permanent planting), a third of eggplant, and a forth of lettuce. The squash will gradually be allowed to fill in around the

❧ Chef Marc Meneau of Vézelay
designed an original potager in which
each square bed is divided into four
triangles, with the center higher than
the outside edges. Endless variations of
texture, height, and color are possible
within this basic design.

eggplant and cover the lettuce space as its contents are harvested.

The test gardens of the magazine *L'Ami des jardins* are situated in Normandy. Philippe Ferret has been experimenting here for almost a decade, not only with the best varieties of vegetables for home gardeners but with a wide range of decorative possibilities. In 1994, he proposed to his readers two models for beginning gardeners, two plots divided by paved paths into four equal sections, one about 20 feet square, the other about 30. Paving for both is laid out permanently, made of imitation stone, slightly raised with respect to the beds themselves. Here too, the center of each square is a strong focal point, a diamond pattern made with paving stones for the small one, a raised stone platform for the larger. Within these strong patterns, plantings evolve throughout the season, ever changing. The smaller the garden, the simpler should be the design.

Ferret knows that garden outlines are established above all by paths. While some gardeners of the organic school may change them from year to year, in many vegetable gardens the paths are laid out once and for all. Materials for best effect are chosen from local sources, and each region of France has its typical stone—dark granite in the center, golden or white limestone in the south, black volcanic stone in the Auvergne, and so on. Flat roof tiles can also be used for paving: The south is famous for its terracotta tones, the north for its slate, the center of France for stone slabs called *lauzes* or *laves* according to the region. Many home gardeners buy up materials from a local demolition company and lay out their paths themselves, in some cases composing inventive mosaics out of pebbles

✣ *Top:* A Provençal designer, Dominique Lafourcade, uses smooth Rhône River pebbles and brick for the paths of her herb garden, outlined in dwarf box.

✣ *Center:* The sparkling white paths of the Château de Villandry use sand from the Loire River, also with low box edging.

✣ *Right:* At La Massonnière, cobblestones provide solid path material, while colorful begonias strengthen the line of box under the apple cordons.

✣ *Opposite:* An Ardèche country garden paved with *lauzes*, or slate slabs, once used as a local roofing material.

and tile fragments in the heart of the garden, near a bench, or in any spot where paths meet and broaden. Mixing materials—pebbles, tiles, stone, or brick—can be confusing rather than enriching, however. Much depends on the size of the garden and on the local traditions of rural architecture.

Various experts in the French gardening press advise on paths 2 feet wide for frequent walking, but 3 feet or more where a wheelbarrow must pass. Rotary cultivators require wide spacing and broad access paths. At the Château de Villandry, many paths are only 2½ feet wide with a covering of fine white *mignonette* sand from the bed of the Loire River. Organic gardeners in France often prefer hand cultivation with one of the *fourches-bêches*, or digging tools designed not to turn the soil over but only to aerate it. This allows for much narrower spacing than in gardens that must allow passage for the conventional rotary tiller, although room for a wheelbarrow is still a necessity. Of course there exist also many machines smaller than rotary tillers that can be used in various systems of intensive planting where the beds are small or irregularly shaped.

Paths can add great beauty to the garden. Where less "noble" materials (like cement blocks) are used, creeping thymes and sedums can soften harsh textures and joints. Gravel paths are usually kept clean with weedkillers or, more ecologically, with a buried sheet of plastic. Grass, like chamomile and other low-growing herbs, can be mowed regularly, but it is an illusion to think the herb paths will not need regular hand-weeding. For grass or herb paths, some sort of vertical edging should be buried or half-buried (upright bricks or tiles with points in the air, or underground metallic bands) to prevent the path plants from spreading in among the vegetables. Problems of water runoff and drainage are essential considerations also, whatever the choice of materials, particularly at a time when so many regions of both Europe and America have been subject to heavy rains and even flood damage.

BORDERS AND EDGERS

One of the most creative possibilities in potager design is the use of plants as edgers along paths or around beds. These can be temporary (parsley, red or green basil, red-leafed lettuce) or permanent (the striking, dark, evergreen outlines of dwarf box, germander, hyssop, or rosemary).

Evergreen edgers should be chosen carefully so that they do not prove too competitive with the crops they enclose. In some decorative potagers, the evergreen outline dominates to such a degree that the vegetables serve merely as brightly contrasting fillers, like different colored sands in neoclassical parterres. Such is an elaborate potager designed by Rosemary Verey in southern France, where dwarf box lozenges make a pretty design around red oak-leaf lettuce, alpine strawberries, or ornamental cabbage. But in this case, there is a productive potager for household use hidden around the corner.

Dwarf boxwood is decidedly the most popular edging plant used in formal French potagers, although slow growing and prone to snails. It does create a firm, dark line that allows for overspilling exuberance within, as at the Priory of Salagon and a private garden in Provence, around a grand herb border. Its solid blocks of vegetation can also create interesting shadows.

Potager edging is above all a kind of foliage gardening, even though flowers (pink balls on the chives, purple spikes on the sages and lavenders) can add brilliant color for a time. All sorts of possibilities for leaf colors and textures can be envisaged here, many of which are listed on page 174. Combinations are endless: Purple-leafed sage (*Salvia officinalis*) is nicely offset by the silver and pewter of lavenders and helichrysums, for example. The same family of herbal sages has three-toned and yellow-spotted varieties, of which the latter is perhaps the most reliable. The santolinas also offer several foliage textures and tones of either silver or deep green, and are very popular in France for vegetable garden edging, less formal and more rustic in mood than box but, at least the silver varieties, equally accepting of heavy and regular pruning. Indeed they require cutting back more than once a year.

For darker tones, dwarf box is a more expensive but very popular alternative, and is by far the most commonly used potager edging in France. Some gardeners judge, however, that boxwood encourages snails, and prefer rosemary or winter savory. An effect similar to that of box can be obtained by using dwarf honeysuckle (*Lonicera nitida*) that will also need careful clipping, or the brighter tone of evergreen *Euyonymus microphylla*.

All these plants make strong, solid lines. Their best effects come from repetition and variation within the general plan. Their pattern should be easily readable in its repetitions, hence not too complicated.

Edgers also gain from being set off by the crops grown right next to them. Feathery, bright green carrot foliage rising above red oak-leaf lettuce or fine-textured bush thyme creates a most pleasing layered effect that can be repeated on any scale: red atriplex behind globes of lavender, or corn rising behind a line of rhubarb chard. Certain vegetables and fruits can themselves be used to good effect as edgers and outliners; many types of sweet and hot peppers are extremely decorative. Strawberries make good strong lines and their proximity to paths means easy picking, even for casual visitors; but like many "permanent" edgings, they are best moved every three years or so.

Edging provides a golden opportunity to practice companion planting, and obviously many medicinal and aromatic plants can be used here for both beauty and practical reasons. Similarly, many flowers can be used as edging—the most obvious are marigolds, famous for their effects on nematodes in the soil, and cheerful as a border outline next to vegetables. Pinks (*Dianthus*) can also be used, or catnip (*Nepeta*). The possibilities are endless.

Few edging plants behave as reliably as furniture though marigolds come close, once established. Most plants evolve throughout the season and will need cutting back, a job the gardener should remember when making a choice. Will they continue to grow in volume until the end of the season, or will they need cutting back almost to the ground halfway through? This question is important also because one of the main advantages of edging plants in potager beds is that they may hide transition periods—the half-dug early potato bed, for example, to be followed by a planting of mustard (used as green manure), or mâche (a fall and winter crop) not yet big enough to show. Shrubby evergreen edgings also keep the garden alive in winter, and are especially beautiful when outlined with snow.

The ultimate use of edging plants to create outlines is surely the practice of some château gardeners who write their names or those of their properties in a mixture of lettuce, herbs, and flowers. At the Château de la Chaize in the Beaujolais, various salad greens, santolina and *Sedum spectabile* spell out a vast alphabet on the slope between the vegetable garden and the formal French parterre, presenting a striking display from late summer until winter. Such effects imply a lofty or distant viewpoint, and also a sense of grandeur, which is, after all, one of the sources and inspirations of decorative French vegetable gardening.

❧ Paving maintains order—even in gardens where the vegetables tend to go their own way.

Enclosure

Successful vegetable gardening requires maximum sunshine and protection from prevailing winds—a careful combination of exposure and enclosure. This implies either a wall or hedging along at least one side of the chosen plot, if not along all four sides, as in traditional French potagers. Both walls and hedging offer the additional advantage of supporting climbing fruits and vegetables, increasing the productive surface of the garden as well as its visual variety and charm. La Quintinye took it for granted that walls were essential for a potager. In Mediterranean France, however, a different balance of enclosure and exposure results from the centuries-old use of hillside terraces, whose strong lines and severe architecture can have great visual appeal.

WALLS

The earliest French potagers (monastery or abbey gardens) were entirely enclosed to provide protection both from intruders and the weather. A typical arrangement, laid out around a central fountain, combined the production of vegetables, medicinal herbs, flowers for altar bouquets, and fruit. Such plans are described in Carolingian times by Brother Walfrid Strabo, in the first western European

practical garden treatise. The author writes lyrically about his vegetables, watered by morning dew, caressed by the moon at night. Such a garden, called *Hortus conclusus,* was a form of paradise garden and its religious symbolism was later transformed by medieval love poets, for whom the image of the fortified, secret Eden took on a more sensual meaning.

Many French gardeners today experience walled gardens as a kind of private paradise—without symbolism, but still with a sense of poetry. The writer Colette recalls her childhood in a village house, where her mother gardened in a backyard surrounded by neighbors on all sides. What ill wind could cross over the high row of espaliered fruit trees, she asks, or that other wall topped with flat tiles, weathered with sedums and lichens, that the local cats used as a highway? This was a special place

❧ *ABOVE:* **Old French potagers often have a second, half-hidden entrance—a simple, narrow door that has stirred the imaginations of writers such as Marcel Proust and André Gide, and also delights children.**
❧ *OPPOSITE:* **French potagers use both stone walls and hedging to enclose and shelter tender vegetables. Here at La Massonnière, a border of pink, white, and red cleomes thrives in the protected microclimate thus created.**

🌿 *ABOVE:* **Dahlias on fire bring out the soft flame tones of the walls at the Château of Miromesnil, which have particularly fine texture and color. This garden has 640 linear meters (about 700 yards) of such walls.**

🌿 *OPPOSITE:* **In Provence, a potager designed by Rosemary Verey lies next to a cutting garden laid out by Ryan Gainey, both enclosed by highly decorative wood fencing with a rhythm all its own.**

where children never fought, where animals and people became gentle, where, for thirty years, a husband and wife lived peacefully without ever raising their voices. Her mother, she recalls, maintained daily dialogue with the neighbors beyond the enclosure on all points of the compass, tossing over a bouquet of violets to the lady eastward, or trading tools with the gentleman to the north. The easterly direction, though, did hold the peril of treacherous winds.

Château potagers were enclosed in another spirit: for weather protection, of course, but also to set them off from the purely ornamental parterres, considered more noble because nonutilitarian. Only in the parterres were distant prospects on the countryside integrated into the garden design, these being deemed unnecessary and inappropriate for a potager. The latter's connections with the outside world were afforded by a woodlot along one side, or by the imposing silhouette of the château itself rising above the line of the wall, in the near distance. Both simply increase the sense of enclosure from within the potager itself. So it is still at the wonderful Château de Saint-Jean-de-Beauregard near Paris, where fairs are held twice a year for fruits and vegetables, or at Miromesnil in Normandy, where nineteenth-century writer Guy de Maupassant was born. Both of these potagers are very beautiful, full of flowers, fruits, and herbs as well as vegetables, tended by loving owners and devoted gardeners.

Château potagers were relatively large—two acres was considered a standard size. Their surrounding walls contributed to their beauty in a number of ways: first, by their upright contrast to a large, flat surface; second, by their very textures, often weathered, as in Colette's mother's modest garden, with lichens and sedums; and finally by that same pleasing sense of protection from outside tempests that garden walls never fail to produce. Always there is that echo of a secret paradise.

So it is that satisfying symbolism joins up with the most basic practical concerns in the walled or hedged potager, whatever its dimensions. When garden writer Rosemary Verey took inspiration from the Château of Villandry for her famous vegetable gardens at Barnsley House in England, she imagined a low, white,

wooden fence around her more rustic emplacement. A similar structure encloses a potager that Rosemary Verey designed in Provence, a very elegant frame for the elaborate pattern of salads and herbs within. And in the English as well as the Mediterranean example, fencing was also needed to provide protection against the rabbits that proliferate outside the garden.

Philippe Ferret, in his experimental gardens in Normandy, regrets the lack of weathered stone walls that add so much beauty to the gardens of that region. He has found alternatives that are both practical and beautiful, however. Ferret makes much use of woven, wooden slatted structures called claustras that are purchased

much use of woven, wooden slatted structures called claustras that are purchased as ready-made walls, light to move and easy to set up. The effect is immediate, there is no root competition, and the structures are strong enough to provide support for climbing vegetables. They have good, natural color and texture, and are discreet but pleasing to look at. Quality and prices vary, however, says Ferret. One should examine several possibilities before choosing, as they will need replacing from time to time.

If stones or bricks cannot be used, garden walls can also be constructed with cement blocks or with wire netting, though these materials should be covered quickly with a curtain of greenery. Wood fencing is rare in many regions of France today, where stone is cheap and more readily available. There is a tradition of wood fencing, however: In Charlemagne's time, log palisades were common, as were braided branches around upright poles. Some inventive gardeners, using similar principles, still weave small lengths of fencing out of wicker rods or willow shoots. In the southwestern province of Landes, heather branches are sometimes used this way.

☙ *ABOVE & OPPOSITE:* **Provençal garden designer Dominique Lafourcade enters her potager through a wooden gate, the circle of which frames the terracotta-tiled roof of the garden shed at the far end. Riviera designer Bruno Goris enters his by pulling back an old iron bedstead. Its compartments have walls of hop hornbeam** *(Ostrya carpinifolia)*, **which grows wild nearby.**

Nowadays mail order catalogues offer a rather different, standardized modern version of wooden fencing. This choice, like that of modern paving materials, appeals by its price and practicality, but it runs the risk of conflicting with the strong regional styles of each individual French province. The most beautiful vegetable gardens generally take their inspiration for any constructions from local traditions, using materials that have served for centuries, not all of which are expensive. In southern France, fast, temporary protection is often provided by sheets of bamboo reeds tied together, called *canisses*. Farmers grow stands of these giant reeds *(Arundo donax)* along the roads near their irrigation ditches; the bamboo provides stakes for supporting tomatoes and other vegetables and the raw material used in the manufacture of these screens, which are available already assembled at supermarkets and garden centers.

Walled gardens usually have gates, and these afford many decorative possibilities. Seventeenth- and eighteenth-century château gardens usually have gates with elaborate wrought-iron lacework. In a recent potager designed by landscape architect Dominique Lafourcade, the gate is made of wood painted in a soft gray-green, its lower half solid, an upper circle framing the garden beyond. It

book about garden gates, suggests using pale tones for a construction that will be seen against a dark background, like an evergreen hedge, and dark materials or paint to be silhouetted against the sky or a pale wall beyond.

Where no gate is required to keep out animals, or simply for appearance, an arch over the entrance path, part of the surrounding hedge, may prove very effective. Hornbeam hedging shaped into arches connects the potager garden rooms in the large domain at La Massonnière. Bruno Goris preferred hop hornbeam (*Ostrya carpinifolia*), which grows wild locally, to enclose the four much smaller compartments of his Riviera potager. The effect is to increase even more the sense of treasures to be unveiled.

LIVING WALLS

Hedges, of course, provide the main alternative to garden walls. The question arises: Which is better, hedging or walls? The former takes time to grow. Crops may be poorly protected for several years before the hedge takes effect. And once the hedging plants are mature, their roots may compete only too successfully in drawing water and nutrients from the vegetable beds nearby. Practical garden books generally advise hedging only for large gardens, where a broad path can separate the enclosure from the precious growth it protects. And certainly in such cases, a dark green curtain beautifully sets off the wealth of color and the shapes of the vegetables, just as elsewhere it serves as a neutral backdrop for colorful mixed borders. The long, rectangular garden of chef Marc Meneau in Burgundy has a tall, smooth, dark expanse of thuya along one side, facing a lower stone and brick wall opposite. At regular intervals along the latter, earthenware pots are planted with squash and pumpkin that drape and color the already picturesque wall all summer long. The two sides provide a most pleasing contrast of textures and tones—the one dark, tall, and uniform, the other bright, lower, and in constant change. At the far end, a grapevine and a wisteria largely cover the shorter cross wall, where an arch opens into the service area beyond.

🌿 Hedging used on both sides of paths will appear, from certain angles, as layered bands of varying heights, a wonderfully effective frame for the lighter tones and more billowing shapes of vegetables, as here at the Château de Galleville.

But even in more intimate gardens, some owners are willing to sacrifice productivity for beauty by using densely

planted hedging, as in the example of Bruno Goris's Riviera potager.

Philippe Ferret also uses hedging. He particularly likes hornbeam; it is not too invasive and, although not evergreen, its leaves stay on the branches far into the winter. When they finally fall, they make good compost. They shelter a number of beneficial garden insects, and they have a natural look, a bit old-fashioned.

At the Landscape Conservatory of the Château de Chaumont near Blois, Belgian designer

❧ *ABOVE:* In the potager of chef Marc Meneau, pots spaced at regular intervals along the top of the wall are planted with squash and pumpkin. The vines tumble gracefully down among the wisteria foliage as they grow.
❧ *OVERLEAF:* At the Château de Galleville in Normandy, multilayered hedging and formal row planting create patterns as rich as those at the Château de Villandry, but at the same time there remains both a greater sense of enclosure and a more human scale.

Jacques Wirtz chose beech hedging to outline the thirty bell-shaped experimental gardens that change yearly, allowing young and established landscape designers to display their styles and to experiment with new ideas. Each thus starts with the same basic plot, surrounded by a neutral hedge pruned to about 4 feet in height.

At least one potager is featured in each year's display.

Since the mid-1970's, there has been a movement to establish mixed fruit and flower hedges, led largely by a man named Dominique Soltner with the support of the organic gardening community. His aim was to combat the type of suburban hedging that was encroaching more and more on rural communities, a rigid barrier of cypresses (usually the blue Arizona variety) or thuya, surrounding a stretch of lawn. This model tends to be copied all over France, ignoring regional traditions and architecture. The houses and gardens enclosed are equally standardized, invariably including a weeping willow and a clump of forsythia, rarely vegetables.

❧ *ABOVE:* **In many châteaux potagers, fruit trees are trained against high walls, like these fig, peach, and pear trees at La Massonnière. The effect is beautiful and the sun-ripened fruit delicious.**
❧ *OPPOSITE:* **The rambling rose *Rosa longicuspis* tumbles over the garden wall, serving as a backdrop for a statue of Saint-Fiacre, patron saint of vegetable gardeners, made by this garden's owner.**

This is the style of unimaginative suburbia, creating fortress-like, alien enclaves in the rural landscape. Soltner calls such hedging "vegetable concrete."

Dominique Soltner proposes a model of rustic hedging mixing evergreen and deciduous shrubs or trees, producing not only wind protection but flowers and fruit as well. Its inspiration comes from old-fashioned rural hedges that, in some areas of France, are traditional. Its composition varies from region to region. The planting method is simple and economical, using very young plants purchased in quantity and set out in plastic or biodegradable sheets that act as mulch for the early years. Soltner has designed a series of different hedge plans, with spacing and planting carefully noted, for northern or southern climates, for acid or alkaline soils, for humid or dry sites, for clipped or freeform borders, for tall field or garden hedging. A northern mix might include three or four of the following: abelia, colutea, buddleia, box, wild dogwoods, cotoneasters, elaeagnus, holly, mahonia, pyracantha, lilac, privet, hazelnuts. A southern example for alkaline soil, in a place that cannot be irrigated but where the soil is deep and fertile, alternates gleditsia with carob and almond trees; or hackberry, Montpellier maple, and pistachio; or large-leafed lime, honey locust (*Robinia acacia*), and privet. A site likely to be flooded in winter might use poplar, white willow or wicker tree, and thorny wild plum. The combinations are endless and inventive, and carefully thought out. Their success has been such that many big commercial nurseries now offer special series of rooted tree cuttings and reproduce Soltner's models in their catalogues.

NOURISHING WALLS

Vegetable gardens in France as elsewhere make the most of their enclosing structures to help produce food. And if hedges can provide fruit, walls offer wonderful support for climbers of all description. Grapevines traditionally find their way up walls onto trellises along one side of the vegetable plot. Their pivoting roots provide very little competition. Among the best-loved, old-fashioned varieties are the Muscat de Hambourg and the Chasselas de Fontainebleau. Today, kiwifruit is often grown as well as or instead of grapevines, even in such classical surroundings as the walled gardens at the Potager du Roi in Versailles. But the kiwi vine is certainly more voracious than the old-fashioned grapevine. Climbing blackberries of various sorts are also readily available, including the giant thornless kind that puts out shoots of 9 to 15 feet yearly. Very vigorous, they produce large, decorative fruit in late August.

In one elegant formal garden in Provence, landscaper Dominique Lafourcade designed two long pergolas, running a good hundred yards along each side of the large ornamental garden. Wanting, however, to keep a rustic tone and echo the nearby potager, she has covered these not only with the wisteria, rambling roses, and table grapes that traditionally run along the front of Provençal farmsteads, but also with blackberry vines. As they visit, strollers can pick berries in one season, grapes in another.

Surrounding walls and hedges can of course support and shelter any combination of fruit-producing climbers and small trees. One garden journalist recommended planting the following against the walls of a typical small garden: four grapevines, a pair of kiwis, an espaliered fig tree of the 'Parisienne' variety, a quince tree, a dwarf apple, an apricot tree, and a cherry tree. These can be enhanced by purely decorative climbers: Wisteria and rambling roses are common but take a lot of room.

❧ Grapevines help cover the long pergolas of the Lafourcade garden, so that strollers can pick and eat as they go. The reflecting disk was intended to keep blackbirds away from the grapes, but in fact adds sparkle to the play of light and shade on the foliage.

ENCLOSURE

Less permanent plantings like the various cucurbits—melons, cucumbers, and squashes—are also easy to train on netting against a solid vertical support. Marc Meneau, near the boutique of his famous restaurant L'Espérance, plants pumpkins all along a 50-yard slope by a driveway. The vegetables are supported by 3-foot-high widths of picket fencing painted green. While they are just beginning to climb, their stems are smothered in a mass of nasturtiums.

Climbing bean plants can easily form a curtain or divider for a new garden. There are many decorative varieties, from the old-fashioned scarlet runner bean (called Spanish bean in France) to the recently distributed hyacinth bean with its deep purple pods. Another chef noted for his vegetable garden, Jean Bardet of Tours, particularly likes a speckled variety called "nun's belly-buttons," but then he is known for his rather ribald imagination.

There are many possible materials to use for enclosing a potager, whether productive or supportive, temporary or permanent. Masonry constructions have the advantage of storing heat in the early spring so that they create special microclimates. In northern châteaux, there is a tradition of having *chartreuses*, garden rooms enclosed by high stone walls for the growing of fruit trees. The Château du Canon-les-Bonnes-Gens in Normandy still possesses an elegant series, where apricots ripen by May and figs in August, a good month before other local orchards.

TERRACES

In Mediterranean France, hillside terracing often replaces walled enclosures. The curves and bends of the hillside provide many protected corners, with the privileged microclimates conducive to good vegetable production, sheltered from cold northern winds. These hillside gardens remain warmer than those in the valley below, which generally have frost pockets.

Many of these tiered stone walls were constructed in the eighteenth century, when the southern French countryside was more densely populated and much new building and planting took place. Vast, steep slopes became arable thanks to the painstaking construction of walls supporting terraces, level by level. Today these picturesque but irregular spaces are almost impossible to farm with modern machinery, and their walls, unless drainage is assured by carefully maintained ditches, tend to crumble here and there. Some of the finest sites have been classified by the government as displaying particular aesthetic and historical interest—for example, at Beaumes de Venise in the Vaucluse department, where vineyards stretch on terraces below a pretty hill town that produces a delicious dessert wine; or at the outdoor museum and terrace conservatory at Goult, east of Avignon. Other terraces now serve for the intensive cultivation of luxury crops; growers use the stored heat and wind protection to get an early start on strawberries, kiwis, dried flowers, tender aromatics, and so on. Farms situated on such terraced slopes always set aside a large, roughly rectangular spot, next to a natural spring, for growing vegetables. Many of today's peasant gardens have thus been producing on the same ground, their soil constantly renewed by manure, for two centuries or more. Such a site fulfills all the ideal conditions of shelter and sunshine, of enclosure and exposure, without further need for walls and hedging. At the same time, such gardens fit beautifully into the surrounding countryside. Many are visible from above—just as at Villandry or Versailles—so that their patterns emerge as a whole picture. This effect is difficult to obtain in a walled or hedged garden.

    In terraced gardens, integration into the surrounding landscape is particularly important. Northern French custom makes the potager a secret, separate space, held apart by its walls and hedges. In the south, the vegetable garden may be displayed dramatically like an open drawer on a hillside, one terrace in a series, the others planted with fruit trees or

❧ Mediterranean France has many steep slopes terraced centuries ago for easier cultivation. Their stone supporting walls create sheltered microclimates so that it is unnecessary, as well as impossible, to enclose such gardens on all sides.

vines. Specific focal points can play an important role in this sort of gradual transition between the potager and what lies outside: one towering boxwood at the end of a rectangular space, or a spreading fig or apple tree that repeats the curve of the hillside beyond. But even a completely enclosed garden will be seen from outside, if only as a long expanse of wall, which by its colors, texture, materials, and volumes should be linked to the landscape beyond.

    Contemporary creations can often play with these variables, turning a flat, open space into whatever the individual imagination creates. Philippe Ferret uses painted wooden tripods to create scale and variety in his two experimental gardens in Normandy. But each of his two plots has a different sense of enclosure: In the smaller one, tall tripods stand at the corners, creating a feeling of intimacy. The larger garden has a tall tripod in its center, with smaller ones on the periphery, for a more theatrical and formal effect. Many combinations are possible, and the balance between secrecy and display will owe much to the individual imagination of each garden's designer. But this balance also depends on proportion, climate, and local custom.

VERTICALS

Vegetable gardening means creating one or more broad, flat spaces, laid out like a beautiful mosaic. But the garden exists in three dimensions and, for best ornamental effect, there must be not only beautiful patterning but contrasts of height. Of course, the fourth dimension—time—dominates all, and will in any case play havoc with the best-laid plans of mice and men. . . .

The garden's walls or hedges may already supply a balancing vertical presence; but these should be strengthened by other uprights throughout the garden, temporary or permanent, planted or constructed. A wide range of possibilities exist: constructions such as trellising, fountains, wells, sundials, tool sheds and other shelters, and even furniture; small trees and shrubs; tall-growing vegetables and small fruit plantations. Some or all of these can come into play in every vegetable garden.

CONSTRUCTIONS

Care must be taken in the placing of verticals with regard to the shade they will cast on surrounding plantings; indeed, this may be a welcome feature and the verticals' reason for being, as in the case of trellising over a path or seat. When Colette first made her legendary garden at the Treille Muscat in Saint-Tropez in 1926, she trained existing vines over arches to shade the main paths, and some of the vegetables, from the hot August sun of the Mediterranean. Jean Bardet, however, the vegetable chef of Tours, finds the magnificent trees that border his garden (including sequoia!) something of a problem, both for the shade they cast and the root competition—a bit too much of a good thing.

In the great châteaux like Versailles, the vertical balance is strengthened forcefully by actual buildings, the whole scene being treated as an architectural composition. *Orangeries,* or winter gardens, play an important role here; these arched buildings once served as shelters for potted trees, not only citrus but also figs, peaches, and other fruits, which were valued that much more for being produced out of season thanks to the climate control that these constructions permitted.

Today's gardeners use greenhouses in much the same way, and these too can provide height in a garden. Much effort goes into making them both

❧ *Above* **Wellheads commonly stand in one corner of any traditional French potager. Many are made from stone or brick and wrought iron, others using wooden beams with small roofs. Today most are more decorative than practical.**
❧ *Opposite:* **Upright sundials come in all shapes and materials, nowhere more gracious than in this weathered stone version at La Massonnière, carefully placed along a main axis.**

practical and aesthetic at the same time, though here again, château gardens sometimes have an advantage in possessing beautifully designed nineteenth-century greenhouses of vast proportions. These can be impossible to maintain today. An elegant example at the Château de Roussan in Saint-Rémy-de-Provence has been repaired only at its south end, which now shelters a permanent table display of succulents, while the north end brims over with hardy perennials in colorful array. At the Château des Pêcheurs in central France, the lovely iron frame is maintained without glass as a support for rambling roses. On the other hand, chef Jean Bardet still uses the beautiful, mid-nineteenth-century greenhouse extending along one side of his potager, clearly visible from his dining room, to start off eggplant, squashes, rhubarb chard, ornamental cabbage, different basils and . . . his fifty-odd varieties of tomato. At the far end of Bardet's vegetable garden, a much more intimate trelliswork kiosk lets the stroller sit and look back at the greenhouse through the garden. In the center of Bardet's herb garden, a simple set of four iron chairs around a table, all painted green, provides effective vertical contrast to the geometries of the surrounding beds of aromatics.

The potager of the Château de Saint-Jean-de-Beauregard has another type of greenhouse, also common in château gardens. A base of solid, brick walls contrasts with the transparent, peaked glass roofs. One greenhouse contains nothing but table grapes (the Chasselas de Fontainebleau and Alphonse Lavallée varieties). Saint-Jean-de-Beauregard also has one of the rare remaining examples of the "fruitier," a house for the storage of grapes with their stems in bottles, a method developed in the mid-nineteenth century which preserved the fruit until Christmastime.

Dominique Lafourcade, a professional garden architect in Provence, has designed a greenhouse in steel, painted with the soft gray-green now seen so frequently in French gardens for decorative detailing. It lies along the north side of a symmetrical, two-part vegetable garden. The path providing the main axis of the garden leads to an ocher-toned shed with a green-tiled roof. These owners felt it worthwhile to invest in a small, permanent building rather than a makeshift shelter for pots and tools, and made it a focal point (seen from the entrance gate) rather than hiding it away on one side. In a sense, their logic is that of the château owners of earlier times, on a much smaller scale: Everything in the garden is architectural and must participate in the overall design.

Vegetable garden sheds and shelters range tremendously in style from region to region, and according to the type of garden. Home gardeners often use salvaged materials to invent their own devices. In cities where space has been set aside for rented vegetable plots, some are provided with a tool shed; elsewhere the tenants may have to construct their own, as in the eastern French city of Colmar, where a cheap, easily assembled model in wood has become current. At the other extreme is the community of Villejuif near Paris, where internationally known architect Renzo Piano was commissioned to design garden shelters for urban plots. Visible

from the highway, they look like so many giant butterflies alighting on the land.

Not all upright garden constructions lend themselves to aesthetic presentation. Compost bins are not intrinsically graceful. The most common model proposed in the French garden press is a set of square bins with removable wooden slats for easy access and manipulation; wood ash is

❧ *LEFT:* **The freestanding greenhouses at Saint-Jean-de-Beauregard, famous for their harmonious proportions, sit along one side of the main potager. Saint-Jean produces dozens of varieties of squash and pumpkin, displayed at a great plant fair every autumn.**
❧ *OPPOSITE:* **At La Massonnière, the greenhouse leans against the high stone garden wall, more sheltered than if freestanding but also catching less light.**

RIGHT & OPPOSITE: **Still, open basins, rather than running fountains, allow water to warm up in the sun for use in the garden. While they cannot provide the delightful sound of a fountain, they compensate with beautiful reflections. The stone trough (right) is at the Château de Galleville; the iron drum (opposite) is at the Château of Saint-Jean-de-Beauregard.**

recommended for odor control and general enrichment. Some organic growing methods, like that of Gertrud Franck mentioned earlier, use sheet composting, which makes the use of separate bins unnecessary, at least when a shredder is available.

Vegetable gardens traditionally are located near springs, though today most depend on city water supplies. Where water is plentiful, fountains can provide beautiful vertical focal points. And yet, for some reason, this is rarely done. Round basins with only slightly raised edges are by far the most common choice—perhaps to allow the water to warm up in the sun before being applied to the vegetables? Upright wellheads are frequently seen, however, topped by lovely wrought-iron structures or even by little tiled roofs, and these can add character to the potager. More prosaically, near the house where Colette spent her childhood, a water pump stood at the heart of the garden. It was sheltered by a gingko tree. In Colette's fond memories, the most powerful vertical of this small, walled domain was her mother's figure, standing rooted amid its luxuriance.

Other gardeners draw the eye upward with sundials or weather vanes. A papal bull of the tenth century apparently required all church roofs to sport a rooster weather vane in honor of Saint Peter. Today some gardeners set the rooster in the garden, attached to a tall pole, for an effective garden sculpture. Garden expert Bruno Goris, in his mountain garden behind Nice, received as a gift a weather vane of painted metal depicting him in his broad straw hat, followed by his faithful dog. Others, like Madame Rolando at the Riviera restaurant Villa Saint Jean near Grasse, keep to the traditional rooster, but set the bird directly on the ground where he crows among the oak-leaf salads. But there of course he sacrifices the effect of verticality for that of surprise.

An unusual decorative object that is vertical—insofar as it must be hung from something tall—is a set of chimes, with or without reflecting mirrors. Though these may be intended to keep birds away from fruit, they can add a delightful, discreet music on a windy day, and serve to draw the attention of visitors to unsuspected corners—not only among the vegetables, of course.

☽ *ABOVE:* **The owner of this garden makes his own ornamental plant labels from zinc, according to the methods of nineteenth-century craftsmen. This one refers to a David Austin rose, created in 1973.**
☽ *OPPOSITE:* **Many châteaux gardens use topiary towers to provide vertical accents. Here at Villandry they rise from a bed of *tradescantia,* near an arbor decked with grapevines.**

Finally, not least among decorative vertical constructions stands the traditional scarecrow, an obvious vehicle for the imagination of all the family.

TALL AND SMALL TREES

In the rural landscapes of the south of France, cypress hedges rise above fields of vegetables, completely dwarfing in scale the low, espaliered apple and pear orchards they protect, all the more dominant when the crop is little winter salads or cabbages. Yet the repeated pattern of this patchwork has become one of the best-loved parts of French scenery. In private gardens in the south, even if cypress hedging is not used to break the force of the north wind, it is rare that the cypress does not appear as punctuation, a dark solid exclamation mark, often set off (in a contrast that Vincent van Gogh particularly praised) by the silvery, floating foliage of an olive tree. An English gardener, Lady Fortescue, lovingly described in her book *Perfume from Provence* the garden she made near Grasse just after World War II, where two tall cypresses flanked her gate, representing Peace and Prosperity.

Château vegetable gardens have special resources for vertical accents in the ancient practice of topiary. Cones and tiered towers appear in grand parterres all over France but also in most intimate properties like La Massonnière near Le Mans, where beautifully sculpted yews and box surround the vegetable garden, their whimsical heads rising over the garden walls.

Fruit trees are perhaps the most popular vertical accent among French vegetable gardeners, though many experts point out the dangers of growing trees in the very midst of vegetable plots. Their roots drain the soil, their foliage provides too much shade. Generally only small varieties are used, often kept two-dimensional in one of the common espaliered forms. These may be against a wall, or freestanding—the apple trees at Monet's garden in Giverny surely count as one of the best-known examples of the latter. But every château potager seems to have its cordons of apple or pear trees along one or more sides of the potager, some very ancient. In his modern experimental garden, Philippe Ferret uses the 'Jubilee' and 'Festival' varieties in this manner, with a row of silver santolina at their feet to edge the path.

Pruning, or one might even say sculpting, such small-growing fruit trees constitutes one of the oldest of French gardening arts. But although it can be traced back to Roman gardens, it is constantly evolving even today. Agricultural research centers are continually coming up with new proposals, such as the "taille Solène" developed in Bordeaux in the 1980's. Here apple trees grow no

taller than vines, and keep only two main branches spread out on wires. Fruit is borne on the tiny shoots that are regularly renewed. The venerable fruit-producing Delbard family is experimenting with a columnar fruit tree. These growers feel that many gardeners today are city people moving back to the country, who no longer know the intricacies of pruning dwarf fruit trees. Simplified varieties therefore become desirable. The columnar dwarf apple 'Polka' marks the entrance to a vegetable bed in Philippe Ferret's experimental gardens.

Many French home gardeners still love to experiment with fruit forms, old and new, however. The 1994 almanac published by the popular gardening magazine *Rustica* gives instructions for some ninety different shapes for the formation of fruit trees, all beautiful if successfully completed, although not all small in scale.

The varieties of fruit trees that can be thus treated increase yearly, owing in large part to international exchanges, particularly with America and Japan. Among the freestanding possibilities, one old type is too often overlooked, though in some regions it turns up as hedging along fields: This is the beautiful quince, an elegant small tree with large flowers and leaves, golden fall color, an almost oriental growth habit, and black bark that make for a striking winter silhouette. Quince trees produce bulbous, velvety, golden fruit like large lumpy pears which make wonderful jams, jellies, and pastes. Cooking gives the fruit a rich reddish-amber tone worthy of the best decorative kitchen displays. And

❧ *Top:* Freestanding plum trees stretch their bloom over a bed of clover, frequently used as a green manure crop in early spring at Saint-Jean-de-Beauregard.

❧ *Center:* Châteaux potagers invariably have fruit cordons, often decades old, some formed as high lacy curtains, others trained as low fences.

❧ *Left:* In Mediterranean France, olive trees combine beauty and practical benefits.

❧ *Opposite:* Quince trees are perfect companions for vegetable gardens—small scaled, undemanding and unassuming, beautiful all year round, and offering abundant harvests.

if that were not enough, custom has it that pregnant women should eat quinces to produce intelligent children!

Many other small trees are suitable for use in potagers; the gardener can choose from among traditional, rare, and newly developed varieties. The medlar (*Mespilus germanica*) should also be better known. Winter-hardy in New England and Alsace, it is closely related to the pear and the hawthorn; it needs sun, however, and well-drained, fertile soil. It has white to blush-pink flowers in spring, curious ruffs of fully developed leaves, twisting branches, and strange, brown fruits an inch wide in late autumn. To be edible, these need to be softened by frost, in which case they can make good jelly. There are beautiful examples of medlars at the Château de Saint-Jean-de-Beauregard near Paris, and in the medieval gardens of the Prieuré de Salagon in Provence, where, besides medlars and quinces, chaste trees (*Vitex agnus castus*) are also grown among the vegetables.

In the south, of course, the pomegranate also makes a beautiful garden tree, with its coppery new growth, showy red flowers, golden fall color, and large red-orange fruit. Another southern possibility is the jujube, or Chinese date (*Ziziphus jujuba*). Its olive-like black fruit can be dried like dates. Its charms are perhaps more discreet.

Mulberries can become big, competitive trees, but if grown in a large pot or tub they can last fifteen years or so and stay manageable. Dwarf varieties exist. The black mulberry has better fruit, but anyone contemplating raising silkworms as a home industry (as was done in large parts of rural France for centuries) would be better off with the white one. Mulberry leaves are broad and luxuriant and provide dense shade, so the trees must be carefully placed. The same can be said for fig trees. In the south, moreover, these wonderful, multitrunked parasols have highly invasive and powerful roots that can demolish any nearby wall in a few years. In the north figs are usually espaliered. Market gardeners near Paris produce some famous varieties like the 'Violette d'Argenteuil'. Louis XIV was particularly fond of figs, especially out of season, and La Quintinye was proud of being able to grow them at

Versailles. In 1687, he delivered four thousand figs for the king's table daily, along with one hundred and fifty melons and thirty varieties of grape. For this feat, however, his famous orangerie was essential.

The old château technique of growing trees in pots and moving them into a shed in winter is still practiced by home gardeners, particularly for citrus fruit. However, producers now propose varieties that can resist lower winter temperatures: Satsumas and kumquats are said to be hardy to 14° F.

The Delbard company has been inventive in introducing not only fruit varieties for the home gardener but also roses, whose design possibilities are infinite, even in the vegetable garden: as standards, in

❧ *ABOVE & OPPOSITE:* The Lafourcade garden
in Provence was designed on a broad, flat
terrain, a site unusual in the hilly south.
Vertical contrasts are provided by the twin
pergolas along the sides and an effective use
of terracotta pots in all sizes. One of Madame
Lafourcade's most original effects comes
from planting olive trees in huge jars, here
seen against the purple spikes of Russian sage,
part of the box parterre, with the grapevines
behind. The potager lies just beyond.

hedging, or on trellising. Contemporary French landscape designers give much play to roses as groundcover and hedging; they regard standards as a mite old-fashioned—though not old enough for nostalgia, however! At Villandry, bright red standard roses are much admired for their vertical contrast among the multicolored squares of vegetables. Each of the four main sections of the potager has thirty-six of these. In family potagers, the rugosa family is often favored since it is easy to grow in most climates, and provides large hips rich in vitamin C that make good jam.

Among small trees and shrubs that do not produce edible fruit, but are suitable as accents in a vegetable garden, the choice is endless. Garden writer Jean Le Bret recommends, for example, the following, which can kept kept under 6 feet in height: *Ulmus parivfolia* 'Geisha', *Caragana arborescens* 'pendula', or *Salix integra* 'Hakuro Nishiki'. The silver weeping pear is also an attractive choice, and the more rustic *Colutea* with its reddish seed pods also has much to recommend it. More commonly grown shrubs and small trees that are not too invasive for plot corners or central accents include box and bay laurel (kept small by clipping), the smaller viburnums, fuchsia, and small hydrangeas.

TALL VEGETABLES AND FLOWERS

Vegetables themselves can provide vertical accents in the potager design, and indeed few gardens are without some examples of this. Some vegetables grow tall naturally, others need support. In the former group, artichokes and the even larger cardoons make striking silver fountains that cannot go overlooked in any setting. The former are tender, but the latter survive in all regions of France. Unfortunately, both may die back in midsummer and look shabby for several weeks; for that transition period they must then be shielded from view by some other planting. Cardoons are often grown in English gardens for purely decorative reasons in the back of mixed borders, but in France, their stalks are blanched and cooked for the table, with bone marrow in the Lyons area, with anchovy sauce in the southeast.

Jerusalem artichokes or sunchokes (*topinambours* in French, *Helianthus tuberosus* in Latin) and sunflowers both provide great masses of bright yellow and are traditional features of peasant or "cottage" gardens in France. Claude Monet painted a whole wall of sunflowers in his garden at Verneil (before Giverny). French garden writer Michèle Lamontagne suggests setting out small plants of tomatoes and sunflowers together, so that the former may use the latter for support. Colette described sunflowers as having "hearts like cakes of black enamel" and grew them draped with sky-blue morning glories. Colette also liked (following her mother's example) what she calls *batons de Saint Jacques,* or kniphofia, and canna lilies, just to add more height and color. Another tall-growing old favorite in or around vegetable gardens is the old-fashioned, single-flowered hollyhock. In France as elsewhere, the 'Nigra' variety, such a dark red as to be almost black, has found many admirers lately. Hollyhock flowers, infused in simmering water, are said to make a good hot tea.

Colette also grew amaranth, which has drawn attention in recent years as a food source that may help to combat the problem of hunger in underdeveloped countries. It too is a tall-growing and colorful plant, readily available in most French seed catalogues; the specialist nursery Baumaux offers some fifteen varieties. Collector and author François Couplan proposes *Amaranthus retroflexus* (redroot) as his first choice as a vegetable; it grows up to 3 feet high and has reddish stems. But the ornamental *Amaranthus caudatus* (love-lies-bleeding) is used for its high-protein seeds, whereas prince's-flower (*Amaranthus hybridus Erythrostachys*), 5 feet tall with clusters of reddish brown flowers, can be used for both its leaves and its seeds.

Asparagus commonly is planted in a row along the edge of vegetable gardens, since it can occupy the same ground for many years. Few plants are more decorative during the summer and autumn, when its strong, green plumes gradually turn to old gold. Though it takes three years from planting to the first crop, most gardeners find asparagus well worth waiting for. Some prefer the green, others the violet-white varieties, and now some catalogues are offering a purple one, 'Jacma pourpre'. Even a single asparagus plant can make a compelling accent, though it will not provide much food. It is used this way in the potager designed by Rosemary Verey in Provence. Asparagus sometimes sows itself, its feathers suddenly emerging among other plants, often with happy results.

Rhubarb counts as one of the garden's most colorful and strongly architectural features, so much so that some gardeners place it squarely in the flower beds. A perennial that will also remain in the same place for several years, rhubarb provides great mounds of fat, reddish-tinged leaves. These contain much higher concentrations of oxalic acid than the stocks and should not be eaten, hence they should not be exposed as a temptation to passing children. The liquid produced by boiling rhubarb leaves in water (in a proportion by weight of 1 to 10), when poured into the planting holes of cabbage transplants, is reputed to help prevent cabbage-root hernia.

Cabbage family plants offer a wide variety of heights and volumes as well as colors. Among those that stand out, so to speak, the big broccolis can be highly decorative, especially the lime-green seashells of

☙ *ABOVE:* **Among the plants that can rise in contrast to a spread of low vegetables, rhubarb is popular because of its strongly designed foliage and colorful stalks.**
☙ *OPPOSITE:* **Artichokes provide even more powerful foliage patterns in nuances of silver, and these strange erect buds, if left to flower, become huge purple thistles.**

Romanesco, or the little red mushrooms of the purple, cut-and-come-again varieties. Brussels sprouts also make towers in red as well as green. But some older varieties of cabbage can reach up to 6 feet or more: The Sarth cabbage and the black Florentine variety grown at Salagon are examples.

Also in the Salagon garden, along a side wall, is a wide range of small shrubs, all known to have been common in medieval gardens, and all possible accent plants where climate will allow: caper bushes, azaroles (a kind of hawthorn), fennel, bush thyme, spiky spurges, rosemary, asphodeline, and acanthus.

Some plants are too spindly to be used on their own but can make a strong statement when grouped in stands. So it is that Philippe Ferret uses a thick row of dill as a sort of small hedge in midgarden.

The same is true of the less common but still available *Atriplex hortensis*, orach (in French *arroche*), the red-leafed variety in particular. Capable of reaching 6 feet in height, it makes a striking accent in the midst of the vegetable tapestry. In chef Marc Meneau's garden in Burgundy, winter leeks left to flower make a stunning contrast with newly planted orach. The company Biau Germe, specializing in organically grown seeds, carries it regularly in France, as do a number of American counterparts. Those who actually eat orach find its foliage a good sub-

❧ *RIGHT:* Seed catalogues offer endless varieties of runner beans in all colors and lengths, which will fast scramble up any convenient support.
❧ *BELOW:* Sweet corn, well grown, always looks good in a garden. Some gardeners use the stalks as supports for beans.
❧ *OPPOSITE:* Chef Marc Meneau's garden creates vertical accents with staked tomato plants, red orach, leeks and onions allowed to flower, bronze fennel, and a small bay tree.

stitute for spinach. For both eating and decorative use, it is best to make successive plantings throughout the season.

In Meneau's garden in Burgundy, where each square bed contains four triangles, the ground at the center is markedly higher than at the outside edges. In the center of each square is a tall-growing plant, a carefully chosen vertical accent. In one growing season, Meneau's upright centerpieces, from bed to bed, include angelica, comfrey, a gooseberry bush, a small bay tree, a black currant bush, and bronze fennel. For best effect when seen from the entrance gate, Meneau plants taller things at the end of the garden.

Few French gardeners as yet grow sweet corn for the table. Decorative, multicolored corn seed is easy to find, as are popcorn varieties. Those proposed for eating fresh are mostly nonhybrids sold largely to organic gardeners, who are advised to cook the ears for twenty to forty minutes! The general public meets only ears picked far past their prime and sold under cellophane in the markets. It is not generally understood in France that sweet corn must be treated in much the same manner as fresh peas.

Every American knows that a stand of well-grown sweet corn is a delight to the eye, as well as to the ear when it rustles in the wind. The classic mix of squash, beans, and corn is tricky to achieve in such a manner that the squash gets sufficient light and the beans do not smother the corn; they should be planted only when the corn is already well on its way. Once grown, the stand of corn provides one of the best vertical accents possible.

Among the plants needing upright supports, tomatoes, peas, and beans are surely the most common. Tomatoes in southern France are almost always trained on a structure of bamboo poles or stakes crisscrossed over a horizontal bar. Suckers are carefully nipped and the growing plants guided as attentively as fruit trees. Their height, weight, and growing season can vary tremendously from region to region: The same variety reaching only to 30 inches in the north will eas-

❧ A harmonious scene from the experimental gardens of the magazine *L'Ami des jardins* shows a 'Royal Gala' apple tree and 'Sweet 100' cherry tomatoes rising among chives, curly endive, onions, and the marigold 'Disco orange'.

ily climb 6 feet in the south where it can expand happily for four months or more, instead of two. In northern gardens, tomatoes are often supported simply on wooded stakes, each only 3 to 4 feet high. Some care should be taken to use good-looking ties, such as raffia.

Peas and beans, on the other hand, may have less formal arrangements. Twiggy branches (often from hazelnut bushes) are stuck into the ground, their tops arched inward to form a sort of vegetal vault, soon covered with climbing and clinging green shoots. Beans need strong, long-term support, expecially for the varieties like flageolets (similar to climbing lima beans) or white beans that will be dried for winter use. Here bamboo usually comes into play once again, and often the tepee shape is recommended. Among runner beans that are particularly decorative, the old-fashioned scarlet runner bean (*haricot d'Espagne*) still appears in many gardens, and now comes in several colors. An imaginative potager displayed at the 1994 garden festival in Chaumont-sur-Loire featured a miniature jungle of plants from Southeast Asia (mostly purchased in Paris's Chinatown). Rare oriental squashes and gourds climbed along with chayote up strong bamboo supports set in floating, galvanized tin tubs! This was called "The Island Garden."

At the Prieuré de Salagon in the Alps of Provence, a simple and very attractive support for climbers has been devised from ordinary wooden, flat, diamond-patterned trellising cut into rectangles and nailed between two poles or stakes. Movable and reusable if desired, this can hold up a wide variety of vegetables and perennials.

❦ In the ethnobotanical gardens of the Prieuré de Salagon in the Alps of Provence, a simple criss-cross wooden trellising supports many different flowers and vegetables—here wild larkspur.

More and more popular today is the tepee tower built from three or four treated wooden stakes tied together at the top and reinforced by wooden crosspieces at the base. A permanent (or at any rate long-lived) structure, this can also be moved from place to place as the garden plan changes. It can be used to support permanent plantations such as vines, ivy, or roses, or, on the contrary, for seasonal plants like runner beans. Philippe Ferret in Normandy has developed a whole system of such supports, painted different colors for different parts of the garden. His two experimental vegetable plots are laid out around these tripods, which are painted blue, made of chestnut stakes, and available in two sizes: roughly 6 feet and 9 feet tall. On these verticals he grows runner beans (the golden-podded variety 'Or du Rhin'), 3-foot-long asparagus beans (*Vigna sesquipedalis*), rare climbing curcubits, nasturtiums and morning glories, 'Mount

❧ *BELOW:* Wooden tripods of differing sizes and colors punctuate the experimental garden created by Philippe Ferret; here the red stems of Malabar spinach (*Basella rubra*) leave room for spider webs.

❧ *BOTTOM & RIGHT:* Tepees made of three bamboo stakes tied together are a classic for beans, often interplanted with squash. But at the Landscape and Garden Conservatory at Chaumont, the farmyard garden created by Eric Ossart in 1993, they are used to support a beautiful display of morning glories.

Everest' strawberries, Malabar spinach (with red-tinged stems and leaves), and cherry tomatoes. At the base of each tripod, geometric shapes made of strips of bamboo are filled in with plants like multicolored lettuce and marigolds to anchor the towers to the general design.

SMALL FRUIT

Like asparagus, small fruit bushes have traditionally been grown in blocks on the edge of the vegetable garden. Like rhubarb, most of these flourish in northern gardens; they can be planted in the south only in partial shade with a lot of water. They are productive and decorative at the same time, if carefully spaced and controlled. Raspberries, gooseberries, blueberries, and currants of all colors are often recommended for the small garden, but can be invasive if neglected.

Some experts recommend growing small fruit as a hedge along one side of the garden, trained between parallel wires, or on a flat row in fan or lyre shapes. But gooseberries and currants, bushes with lobed, fuzzy leaves, also make beautiful freestanding specimens growing 4 to 5 feet tall, pruned into goblets or high-branching shapes like small trees. In any case, all small fruits produce on wood one to three years old, and pruning is useful first to create the shape, then to remove older wood.

Today's choice of small fruit bushes has been enriched by varieties produced in Holland, England, and America. But many of the old French favorites still thrive and have lovely names. Among the gooseberries that grow in clusters: the white Versaille, or the 'Rose of Champagne', or the beautiful 'Gloire des sablons'. Among the gooseberries called "mackerel berries" because, it seems, they used to be served with this fish, some have red, some white fruit. Modern varieties resist powdery mildew better than the old ones. The black currants, or *cassis*, gained fame above all in Burgundy, where they have long been used to prepare a liqueur used with white wine in the preparation of the popular apéritif, the kir. 'Noir de Bourgogne' is still a popular choice.

Quite a number of varieties, here as elsewhere, have disappeared: In 1732, the fourth edition of the *Nouvelle maison rustique* mentioned white strawberries, white, large-fruited gooseberries, and white raspberries. Gertrude Stein and Alice B. Toklas grew such raspberries in their garden in Bilignin between the wars. But they cannot be found today, when only red and gold ones are readily available. At the same time, however, many tasty new varieties have been made available by plant developers such as the Delbard company.

As for blueberries, French gardeners can now choose between the native, low-growing bush types or the tree variety (known in France as the Canadian blueberry), reaching as high as 10 feet tall. The former like shade, the latter full sun, but none will do well in the south except at higher altitudes.

Used as a hedge, or to mark the transition between the lower-growing vegetable plot and the garden beyond, these berry bushes can be decorated further by the addition of a few morning glories intertwined, or clumps of lupin or dahlias

here and there. But in this case, the spacing of the berry bushes must be increased to allow room for comfortable coexistence. Philippe Ferret grows his in wide rows, with an artichoke plant at the end of each. At Salagon, gooseberries are grown in one large square with a strawberry border.

 All of these upright constructions and plantings vastly improve the aesthetics of any decorative vegetable garden, from the tiniest courtyard to a vast landscape. The utilitarian vegetable garden has the unfortunate reputation of being strictly and monotonously horizontal: When Henry James visited the "flat and sandy" Sologne region of France in the 1880's, he dismissed its plain as "prosy" and dull because of its lack of vertical accents: "The wide horizon opens out like a great potager, without interruptions, without an eminence. . . . There is an absence of hedges, fences, signs of property; everything is absorbed in the general flatness." Today's gardeners want to avoid giving just this impression, and luckily they have a broad choice of upright accents. Here as elsewhere, the best effects strike a happy balance between simplicity and variety.

❧ Small fruit bushes traditionally grow in strips along one side of the formal potager, rising above the lower beds to present their ripening fruit to the sun. Gooseberries especially have a splendid color when they catch the light.

THE

BEAUTIFUL VEGETABLES

All vegetables are beautiful, but some vegetables are more beautiful than others. Each has its own shape, color, texture, volume, and taste; each evolves over weeks into something strikingly different from its point of departure, whether seed or purchased plant. In terms of garden design, growing vegetables is largely a kind of foliage gardening, since, with some notable exceptions noted in Chapter 6 and later on, leaves occupy much more space in a potager than flowers or fruit. Flowers usually appear in the decorative vegetable garden as companion plants or aromatics, but the basic tapestry is composed by foliage of different heights and colors.

The choice of varieties will depend, as everywhere, on climate. Many favorites in France are linked to specific localities, much in the manner of cheeses and wines. Towns famous for their onions, for example, include Nard near Paederast, Bellegarde near Names, and Lézignan-la-Cèbe near Montpellier, where even the village name celebrates its favorite vegetable. But hybrids developed recently by government researchers may also bear the name of the station that first produced them, as with the popular tomato from Montfavet. Enthusiasts in France as in many other countries actively work to rediscover and preserve heirloom vegetables. This strong link between tastes and places, between food as it is grown and food as it appears on the table, is one of the most precious characteristics of France's cultural heritage.

Many owners of decorative potagers are also collectors of rare plant varieties, exotic contributions from all over the world. But a beautiful garden can be created out of the most humble, economical, and easy-to-find plants: carrots with their feathery, true-green fountains of leaves, or beets, which in many climates can stay in the ground all winter, adding reddish foliage accents for months on end. In France, perhaps the most commonplace vegetable, used in almost every dish that involves any kind of mixture (much as Americans use celery or onions) is the leek. Few vegetables look more splendid in the ground over a longer period of time. Leeks will grow in every climate and are very undemanding.

❧ *ABOVE:* **One of chef Marc Meneau's compositions features red orach, leeks with round seed heads, fennel in full yellow bloom, red cabbage, young beans, and artichokes.**
❧ *OPPOSITE:* **Ornamental kale, with its nuances of red, green, and white, must be the best-known decorative vegetable, particularly prized throughout the winter for its cheerful and almost Christmas-like colors.**

The following descriptions have been listed according to the type of soil they require or are willing to grow in—rich, medium, or poor. Since any garden planner must group vegetables in this manner from year to year, to allow for a crop rotation that will not exhaust the soil, this organization should help foresee which vegetables can "go together" at any given time. Often they will be members of the same family or type: the root vegetables, for example. But others, such as celery, broccoli, and leeks, all need recently enriched earth, and will do well in the same section of the garden.

Some of the most beautiful vegetables are perennials that need semipermanent situations, either for a few years, like artichokes, or even decades, like asparagus. Finally, special attention is paid to rare varieties that add unusual accents to the garden.

At the end of this book can be found easy-reference lists of potager plants organized by foliage color, height, and other characteristics. Suggestions about companion planting with flowers and herbs appear also in the chapters on those subjects.

☙ At La Massonnière, the potager promises a rich harvest of endive, celery, kale, chard, and tomatoes—far more than the family can eat, but carefully maintained for its beauty.

RICH SOIL

LEEKS: These vegetables are easy to grow from seed but cheap to buy in bunches of fifty or so. Harvested fall through spring (when they bolt), they occupy space over many months. But their striking vertical stalks, reaching up to 2 feet in orderly rows, add strength to any garden design. Their medium green is a good foil for looser foliage like celery or chard. The variety 'Bleu de Solaise' has good resistance to insects, and takes on a bluish tinge with reddish accents in winter.

Leeks, like onions, are often interplanted with rows of carrots, for mutual protection against insects. But they do need room to grow if they are to have maximum effect.

CELERY: Most appreciated in decorative vegetable gardens is the gold-leafed variety. And since a whole long row of celery is more than the average family can consume, it can be largely left intact for best visual effect. An alternative is leaf celery, which can be grown all season without developing real stalks. Leaves can be cut now and then without hurting the garden's design. This solution is helpful only for those who wish to use celery as a seasoning, of course, rather than as a vegetable in its own right. In France, fennel commonly is used raw in salads much in the way Americans use celery.

CABBAGE: This is one of the most decorative plant families for year-round use. Catalogues in France as elsewhere provide a great range of types: pale green and smooth (the *cabus* family in French), or crinkly-leafed and dark blue-green (called *Milan* in French, savoy in English). Sizes also vary tremendously. Red cabbage is an obvious source of color contrast. A row can be used gradually from one end, to keep maximum effect throughout the season. Young cabbage can be

undercropped with lettuces of different sorts, or with low-growing flowers such as sweet alyssum. An often-recommended technique against cabbage moths involves cutting flowering branches of Scotch or Spanish broom to stick in the ground among young cabbage plants. As they must be fresh to be effective, they must be replaced every few days, and therefore can be quite striking in a semiformal arrangement around the plants or in rows between.

Oriental cabbages are now commonly grown in many French potagers, either the chard-like 'pak choy' or the pale green compact lettuce-like variety, both very decorative.

KALE, BRUSSELS SPROUTS, AND BROCCOLI: These again offer a tremendous range of possibilities for all seasons. The kale usually grown for pure decoration, with its froth of deep pink and white among the green, is also edible, if not wonderful. But any one of these plants is inherently strong in structure and subtle in its colors. All are beautiful if allowed to flower. This easily happens in early spring, if all the winter harvest has not been collected. Bees are very grateful at that time of year.

Brussels sprouts come in red as well as green varieties. Purple sprouting broccoli is not well known, but it is delicious and stunning as an accent plant in both spring and fall. The most beautiful broccoli must, however, be the Romanesco, which looks like a chartreuse seashell and has a particularly delicate flavor.

SQUASH FAMILY: Cucurbits compete strongly with brassicas (cabbages) for recognition as the most decorative plant family in the garden. But they fill in slowly only in late summer, and so need fillers and cover crops (see page 175). Squash family plants can be grown on trellises, and cucumbers, especially, do better when vertical. When the plants spread out, their large indented leaves add strong form and, depending on the varieties, cover a lot of ground. The growing fruits should be exposed to the sun—and the eye—by careful cutting back of the exuberant foliage (pinching is recommended by most manuals for growing squashes generally). The fruit can also be placed on terracotta roof tiles or paving stones as they grow both to keep them from exposure to wet soil and to make them more visible. The cucurbits particularly benefit

❧ *Right Top & Bottom:* **Pierre Bourgois, collector of rare and heirloom vegetables, has a conservatory in the Charente-Maritime department in western France, where he grows this 'Golden Hubbard' squash and the 'rouge vif d'Estampe' pumpkin. The latter, like most old varieties in France, bears the name of the town or village which made it famous.**
❧ *Opposite Top:* **The cabbage family (brassicas) includes some of the most spectacular vegetables in the garden at all times of year, including Brussels sprouts, at La Massonnière.**
❧ *Opposite Bottom:* **The cucurbits (cucumber, squash, pumpkin and melons) give their bounty from midsummer to midautumn. But long before the vegetables mature, strongly characteristic foliage provides cover for bare ground.**

from ground-level irrigation such as a drip system provides, and the apparatus will be well hidden by the leaves . . . eventually.

Contrary to popular misconception, French country dwellers have always been great eaters of squash and pumpkin, and there are hundreds of regional varieties: the bright red one of Estampes, the Mirepoix squash, Touraine pumpkins, the musk squashes of Provence, and many more. Now sophisticated chefs have drawn wide attention to this family of vegetables and each has a signature style of pumpkin soup. The summer squashes, which include zucchini and the pattypan types in several colors, are also widely grown and very decorative.

In recent years, a multicolored Japanese pumpkin called *potimarron* in French (belonging to the *Cucurbita maxima* family), averaging about 4 pounds, has become generally available and much appreciated. It has long been grown by organic gardeners for its dense, chestnut-flavored flesh. It is a very good keeper and is said to contain eight times the vitamin A of regular varieties. In the kitchen it can be grated raw like carrot, or cooked as a soup, puree, or soufflé; it can be fried plain or as fritters; it can be used in pies and cakes, even prepared as ice cream and jam.

Chard: This is another fountain shape, but with strong, effulgent foliage. It is grown both for its thick ribs (white, green, or red), which are prepared in sauces like celery but are not eaten raw, and for its leaves, which when tender many prefer to spinach. The most famous variety in decorative gardening is the rhubarb chard. As one writer puts it, a single plant can entirely light up a corner of the gar-

den. Almost every photograph of the elegant kitchen garden of the Château de Villandry features rhubarb chard. If allowed to seed, it may well provide enough small plants in early spring to make a border along one section of the garden. But although it tastes much like the more common green variety, when cooked it keeps a purple tinge that may not please everyone in, for example, a cheese sauce.

FENNEL: Grown mostly in the south of France as a vegetable rich in vitamins, fennel is versatile and beautiful at the table. In the garden the growing bulb is visible above the soil line, a delicate pale green topped by feathery foliage very much like dill. Certain varieties, if planted in rich soil and watered regularly, may be kept from bolting in summer heat. If fennel bolts it is of course also highly decorative, and the bronze variety is

❧ *Above:* Celery root is not normally considered a decorative vegetable, but its delicately cut foliage, fountain shape, and bulb emerging from the ground can be very attractive.

❧ *Opposite:* Cherry tomatoes, both the red globes and the luxuriant foliage, make a good foil for the dainty lacework of white coriander flowers.

❧ *Overleaf:* Chef Jean Bardet of Tours has grown dozens of tomato varieties, some freshly picked ones displayed here. He has even organized tomato tastings, similar to wine tastings.

generally grown for no other reason than its tall stems and foliage, particularly beautiful when backlit. But the bronze is really an herb plant, whose leaves, stems, and seeds are harvested; it is the Florence or bulb fennel, which resembles an anise-flavored celery, that is grown for eating as a vegetable.

TOMATOES: What more succulent vision can there be than vine-ripening tomatoes? French gardeners practice careful pinching and pruning to achieve maximum fruit with just the right amount of foliage. In recent years, they have come to appreciate the American varieties of tiny cherry tomatoes. Standard tomato plants need particularly strong support and can be very decorative indeed. Chef Jean Bardet of Tours claims to have grown 140 varieties of tomato in 1993, but, strapped for time in 1994, had to limit himself to 59. Equally interested in flavor and appearance, he organizes tomato tastings similar to more familiar wine tastings.

EGGPLANT: Plants producing the usual oblong purple fruit are readily available in southern French markets (the most common variety is from Barbentane), but plants producing round or white fruit are also offered. The Baumaux seed company offers an eggplant that is bell-shaped and creamy white with pink stripes! In recent years, eggplant grafted on to tomato stalks have become common: A single plant provides far more fruit than any nongrafted variety, and this can be a considerable spacesaver. Like tomatoes, eggplant must be grown

on supports, and both purple and white ones add unusual color accents to the garden in late summer.

MEDIUM SOIL

BEETS: While the roots now come in a variety of colors, the most decorative for the garden are the old-fashioned, wine-red varieties with their reddish-tinted foliage. Depending on the region, the flat 'Egyptian', or the *crapaudine* variety is recommended for best flavor. Beets are patient vegetables that, once grown, can remain in the ground over a period of weeks without getting woody or otherwise past their prime. In the south, they add a lot to the winter garden. In summer, they mix beautifully with dwarf nasturtiums.

CARROTS: Carrots lend themselves well to interplanting with onions or leeks, which help protect them from carrot fly if these vegetables are already large enough when the carrots are still small. A row of mature carrots provides a strong green stream of foliage not striking in itself but an excellent foil for many other plants with red, yellow, or blue tinges.

ONIONS: These very accommodating vegetables can be harvested when convenient. They serve well as a filler (from sets or transplants), make a nice edging, and mix happily with carrots, salad greens, and tomatoes (but must be kept away from peas and beans). Onions come in several colors, and enough of the bulb is often visible aboveground while growing to add interest—the red Florence or white bunching onions, for example. Most spectacular of all is the Egyptian onion, which forms small, reddish bulblets in the air, several at once proffered jauntily around a single stem.

☙ Garlic stalks have been bent flat to help the bulbs ripen in late June. Other gardeners believe it best to tie the foliage in a knot, which takes more time, and is not necessarily more aesthetic.

GARLIC: This condiment plant looks much like onions while growing and is harvested in late June, so that its space is available for summer crops. Garlic fresh from the garden has incomparable flavor. Two types are commonly planted: white in November, and "rose" or red in the very early spring. Garlic is reputed to protect a long list of plants from pests, particularly roses.

POTATOES: These are not always an asset for the decorative gardener for, although a plot of well-

RIGHT: French vegetable gardeners can be fierce defenders of their favorite potato varieties, now that famous chefs have announced their preferences for the 'Ratte' or the 'Charlotte'. They prefer the yellow-fleshed ones for most uses.

BELOW: Hot peppers awaken the same passions only, so far, in the Basque country of the southwest, though a few varieties, such as the 'Cayenne', are readily available everywhere.

grown potatoes has a good strong dark green color in midseason, by the time they ripen, the foliage has often deteriorated. Many gardeners choose to grow only the fast-developing varieties, some of which are also the ones preferred by the master chefs ('Belle de Fontenay', 'Ratte', 'B.F. 15', 'Charlotte'). The potato plot can be hidden behind a row of chard, for example, until harvested, when it can then be either sown with green manure such as mustard or phacelia, or used as the basis for a winter garden.

SPINACH: This is the wonder plant of organic gardeners who propose it as a cover crop and mulch between rows. It is reliable all season in the north, but fast to bolt in the south, where chard and New Zealand spinach are more reliable.

SWEET AND HOT PEPPERS: France has a number of regional varieties now available only through specialist nurseries, such as the 'Poivre rouge de Bresse' of the Rhône Valley, or the Basque 'Piment d'Espelette'. Otherwise only bell peppers, Hungarian yellow wax, and long hot peppers ('de Cayenne') are commonly found. Little by little the choice is being extended by imports from North Africa and even America, found both in garden catalogues and on the tables of fine restaurants. Few plants are more decorative, with brightly colored fruit on bushy plants; but obviously they need strong sun to thrive.

POOR SOIL

LETTUCE: From what were once hundreds of varieties, dozens survive. Apart from the Boston types most commonly found in shops, the batavias ('Dorée du printemps', 'De Pierre Bénite', 'Rouge Grenobloise') are outstanding for their flavor and color, especially the red or rust-tinged varieties. The cut-and-come-again salad greens, like the oak-leaf lettuces that are available in several colors, make good edgers, though not for an entire season. There are many heirloom varieties in France and others very adaptable to different climates like the 'Gotte d'Or' or 'Reine de Mai' of spring, or the evocatively named 'Grosse blonde paresseuse' (big lazy blonde) of summer. Many of the recently developed red-leafed lettuces, imported particularly from Italy and America, have grown in popularity, among

them the 'Lollo rosso', 'Lollo biondo', 'Casablanca', and 'Salad Bowl' varieties.

Chicories and endives provide other kinds of foliage pattern and an equal range of color. The fine curly endive heads are usually blanched a few days before cutting under an upturned, earthenware flowerpot; one or two heads at a time are covered and checked regularly for snails and slugs. Self-blanching varieties are now also available, though there is a trend toward using greener leaves in salads. These heads can become very big, and they stand cold better than many other types of lettuce.

The salad mixture called *mesclun* is originally a Provençal specialty—the name itself is Provençal and not French. It usually includes endive and often the red, or Italian, chicory (called radicchio in America) that turns color only after frost. There should also be roquette, or arugula, with its deeply indented, dark green foliage and peppery taste. Traditionally this is a mix meant for winter gardens in the south, but now it can be found on menus all year round.

❧ *ABOVE:* The simple garden pea creates beautiful patterns with its angular foliage and swelling pods.
❧ *OPPOSITE:* French salad greens come in every conceivable texture. The endive family (opposite top left) has even more ardent supporters than the looseleaf group (opposite top right). Today, new varieties have come from Italy and America. 'Red Salad Bowl' is particularly popular (opposite lower). In ornamental potagers, salad greens are often allowed to grow tall and bloom. Chicory especially has intense blue flowers.

PEAS: Two types are commonly sold: with either smooth or wrinkled seeds, for early or later sowing, as the latter stand heat better. There are also climbers and dwarf varieties, of course. In northern climates, peas can be grown all summer. In the south, they are a spring and fall crop, and the gardener must foresee a different use of the pea space for summer months. Peas can be beautiful trained on supports such as twiggy branches, or into a low hedge, and of course they enrich the soil with nitrogen as they grow. Some varieties have beautiful purple flowers.

BEANS: These are more interesting, for purely decorative reasons, than peas because they come in so many shapes and colors. The bush plants grown for tiny fresh beans make good fillers since they also enrich the soil and mature fast. Other types are grown on towers or tepees of wooden or bamboo stakes for strong vertical accents. Scarlet runner beans are often recommended for their pretty flowers, but the white-flowering variety has better flavor. If not pinched back, they readily produce shoots 12 feet long.

Among the bush varieties, the yellow butter beans and the purple-podded ones ('Royal Burgundy' is the most commonly found) enrich the gardener's palate and palette both.

PERENNIALS

ARTICHOKES (*CYNARA SCOLYMUS*) AND CARDOONS (*CYNARA CARDUNCULUS*): Both of these require rich soil and a lot of water. Two types of the former are commonly sold in France: the globe, or Breton, artichoke; and the longer, slimmer, purple variety traditional in Provence, where it is often picked very young and stewed. If allowed to flower, artichokes, like cardoons, produce bright purple thistles. Both die back in midsummer in an ugly manner and must be screened somehow. Tall-growing annuals like cosmos or cleome are a help. Both cardoons and artichokes look wonderful in winter in mild climates; in colder regions, gardeners often wrap their artichokes with sheaves of newspaper for frost protection. Some more aesthetic form of bundling could probably be devised—reed fencing, for example.

Cardoons in winter can be left alone for their beauty, or their stalks can be wrapped and blanched for eating. Indeed, with cardoons it is the stem that provides food, not the flower bud as with the artichoke. The blanching stage is not attractive; while it is possible to grow artichokes both for eating and looking, with cardoons you have to make a choice.

RHUBARB: This dies back in winter but is highly decorative in summer, when it is much appreciated both for its large, textured, reddish-tinted leaves and of course the pink-purple stalks that can be turned into pies and jams. Rhubarb grows best in cooler climates, or semishade in the south.

SUNCHOKES OR JERUSALEM ARTICHOKES: Debate rages over the culinary value of this vegetable. The roots (or rather tubercules) were commonly eaten during World War II, and a whole generation in France was discouraged by that memory. In the early seventeenth century, however, Olivier de Serres was proud to grow them and called them "earth pears."

They are variously reported to need rich soil or to grow, most invasively, anywhere at all. This may be a question of climate, as certainly in southern heat without water they perish. They produce tall, dense thickets of small but colorful sunflowers, and make a fast screen or accent.

ASPARAGUS: Beginning gardeners are discouraged by the fact that freshly planted asparagus takes three years to produce, but this is nothing in the life of a garden. Even a small plot of 6 or 8 square yards will give great pleasure in the spring. The beds are hard to maintain weed free, although earth must be pulled up over the shoots early in the season if the shoots are to be blanched, and this destroys small weeds between rows. Various cover and green manure crops are recommended for asparagus (phacelia, salad greens, or pot marigolds) as an alternative to weed killers.

❧ *ABOVE:* **Artichokes are beautiful plants that last for at least several years, if well fed. But they do exhaust the soil, and they can also look tatty for a long spell in hot weather.**

❧ *OPPOSITE:* **Rhubarb is prized for both its decorative and gastronomic qualities, but its foliage is poisonous and should be kept away from small children.**

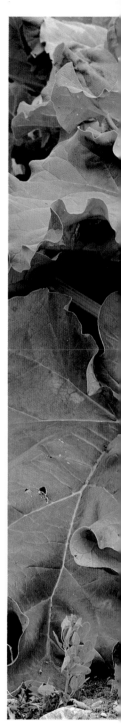

THE BEAUTIFUL
VEGETABLES

After the harvest, the plants must be allowed to ripen their beautiful, tall fronds, which turn bright gold in the fall; after that they must be cut back and destroyed in case they contain beetle eggs.

Marcel Proust much admired the beauty of asparagus being prepared for the table and described his "delight in discovering this vegetable dipped in pink and ultramarine, spikes delicately daubed with mauve and azure changing color little by little down to their feet . . . with iridescences that are not of this world. . . ."

RARITIES AND EXOTICA

In 1892, a book called *Le Potager d'un curieux* was published by La Maison Rustique in Paris, citing the history, culture, and usages of two hundred little-known edible plants. Two of today's experts, François Couplan and Victor Renaud, have written illustrated versions for contemporary gardeners, but each has had to limit himself to a choice of about fifty (not the same fifty). Specialists in other countries have produced similar volumes with guides for both cultivation and cooking. American readers would be surprised to discover butternut squash, broccoli, parsnip, sweet potato, and okra listed as unusual, whereas groundnuts, asparagus bean, burnet, Cape gooseberry, comfrey, purslane, fat hen, herb-of-grace, Good King Henry, rampion, rocambole, seakale, sweet cicely, tuberous glycine, Welsh or Egyptian onion, celtuce, Hamburg or parsley root all count as uncommon, though not unknown, on both sides of the Atlantic. Sorrel, leek, roquette, corn salad, and oyster plant, however, commonplace in France, find themselves listed as continental, gourmet specialties in America.

🌿 France has an active network of collectors of rare vegetables, heirloom varieties, or exotic introductions. The pear-melon (here shown in chef Jean Bardet's garden) belongs to the nightshade family, which also includes potatoes, tomatoes, and eggplant.

Rarity and beauty do not necessarily coincide, of course, and flavor is yet another consideration. Several well-known contemporary chefs have made a point of reviving the culinary reputation of "forgotten" vegetables: Marc Meneau at L'Espérance in Vézelay drew public attention to garden cress (*cresson alénois*), parsnip chervil (*cerfeuil tubéreux*), and red atriplex, or garden orach (*arroche rouge*). Jean Bardet of Tours, like Meneau, has a decorative vegetable garden that may be visited by the public, and one of his recent discoveries is the pear-melon (*poire-melon*), which is in fact a kind of eggplant (*Solanum muricatum*). René Marcon in the Rhône Valley (Saint-Bonnet-le-Froid) cherishes and promotes many old-country treasures like the humble lentil, which grows wonderfully in his mountain climate, not far from the town of Le Puy. Thanks in part to his efforts, the green lentils of Le Puy now have acquired controlled appellation standing.

There are centers of interest in heirloom varieties all over France. At the Jardin Botanique de la Mhotte, for example, gardeners experiment with amaranth, a crop that is often spectacular in color and shape. Work here proceeds in cooperation with the Rodale Institute in Pennsylvania. Plant fairs throughout France encourage exuberant displays of vegetables, familiar and rare, the best-known being held at the Château de Saint-Jean-de-Beauregard near Paris. At the same time, many abbey gardens have been turned into period gardens of medicinal, useful, and edible medieval plants, the Abbaye de Salagon in Provence being a particularly fine example.

The rare vegetables used in specialty gardens for decorative effect include a number of leafy kinds like red orach, also called by the appealing name of *belle dame*. There is also *claytone de Cuba* (in Latin *Claytonia perfoliata*), first cultivated in 1804 in the Jardin des Plantes in Paris, now wild in the north, center, and west of France, along with purslane, which is of the same family. *Claytonia* has white flowers from March to June, grows about a foot high, and is famous for its unusual triangular foliage. Purslane itself is cherished by many gardeners and adds a texture contrast that is visual as well as gustatory (though the ordinary wild variety is an invasive weed).

The cabbage family offers many striking oddities, like the tall perennial cabbage with its rosettes of tender leaves, or the palm cabbage from Italy, or the seakale (*crambé*, or marine cabbage) that grows wild by the North Sea. The young shoots of seakale are specially blanched under large bell jars. But this glaucous plant is perennial, and shoots are harvested only on plants already three years old.

The choice of beautiful and intriguing vegetables is vast, and increases yearly as international exchanges make available more and more exotic varieties. Oriental vegetables are finding their way into French potagers, adding another whole range of shapes, colors, textures, and flavors. French tradition values each variety, one might even say each plant, for its own special qualities, even as these vary from soil to soil and climate to climate. As long as this approach is maintained, cosmopolitan influences will serve to increase the gardener's choices rather than to impose uniformity.

For there is fashion in vegetables as in everything else. Famous British horticulturalist William Robinson visited Paris in 1868 and wrote a book describing the vegetables he found both in public markets and in private gardens. He

❧ The Laotian garden, maintained by immigrant families at the Château of Saint-Paterne, near Alençon, contains many of the oriental vegetables becoming popular all over the country, and also makes good use of flowers in companion plantings.

admired the sweet potato, which had been a favorite of King Louis XV, and was popular again after 1800. By 1868, however, it had become a rarity. He complained that only three varieties were commonly cultivated in France: the red, the yellow, and the New Orleans violet. Robinson would find the contemporary choice sadly impoverished. But if the palette has indeed shrunk, enough beautiful vegetables still remain to give gardeners a wide scope in creating decorative potagers.

FLOWERS

The very idea of decorative vegetable gardening conjures up a vision of gay flowers combined with vegetables. Careful planning of space and proportion works subtly on the eye and mind, but the appeal of floral color is instant, vivid, and compelling.

Such intermingling was once common in French cloister and château plantings. Even after the separation of pleasure from productive gardens during the Renaissance, flowers for the altar or drawing room were still grown along with the vegetables. In contemporary France, when such a mixture is found in a small space, it is usually called a *jardin de curé,* evoking the old-fashioned country priest's garden. Magazines regularly run articles on how to create this idyllic atmosphere in small country gardens today. The style is all charm and intimacy—the romantic vision at its best.

One of today's models, even in France, remains the much better-known English cottage garden. It is often said that the French peasant scorned any cultivation not strictly utilitarian, and certainly he has been far less inclined than the English cottager to experiment with flower gardening. Obviously English tradition is unparalleled in this respect. But many French peasant potagers, in earlier times as now, contained flowers—*pour la patronne,* for the lady of the house. Indeed in many regions the vegetable garden was entirely the woman's precinct, her husband expending his efforts in the much heavier work of the fields. Peasant gardens dotted with bright color certainly existed plentifully enough to inspire nineteenth-century painters such as Vincent van Gogh, who loved their big red roses and dahlias and considered them very poetic. Today, in rural France, the word *jardin* still refers to the vegetable plot. Country people never speak of *potagers*.

Flowers in today's ornamental vegetable gardens are grown either mixed in with the vegetables or in a section of their own, each choice of site having its advantages and drawbacks. As companion plants, they bring many practical benefits as well as beauty to the garden. And, of course, there are vegetables that themselves have beautiful flowers and can be grown for this reason. This chapter concludes with the advice of several French garden writers as to which flowers enhance particular vegetables.

EMPLACEMENT

Whether the gardener wants flowers for pure pleasure or for profit, the first practical question must be: Where exactly should flowers be grown—in a cutting-garden section of their own, in orderly rows between vegetables, as edging, or scattered between vegetables? Should they be allowed to self-sow and indeed choose their own setting?

❧ *ABOVE:* **Seed catalogues regularly advertise double-flowered hollyhocks, but generally only the single blooms can be found in French potagers, their seeds handed on from neighbor to neighbor.**
❧ *OPPOSITE:* **In Eric Ossart's Farmyard Garden at Chaumont different sorts of marigolds intermingle with dahlias and cabbage.**

☙ *RIGHT:* **Wild poppies often invade both fields and gardens, their bright spring note irresistible to many gardeners. But if encouraged, they easily smother any young plants nearby.**
☙ *BELOW:* **Iris lend color to the spring garden of Jean-Paul Collaert, co-author of** *The Lazy Man's Garden.*
☙ *OPPOSITE:* **At the Château of Miromesnil, flowers and vegetables intermingle in neat blocks: sweet corn and lettuce next to phlox, lavatera, and** *Salvia horminum.* **The latter self-sows in many gardens.**

Among experts, opinions vary regarding where flowers belong in the potager. Jean-Paul Thorez, formerly editor-in-chief of the important organic gardening magazine *Les Quatre saisons* and author of numerous books, recommends placing floral borders outside the vegetable plot to draw useful insects, but fears their competition in the heart of the garden. Gertrud Franck, the German writer who inspires many French emulators, insists on flowers and herbs as companion plants right next to vegetables and small fruits: chives among the strawberries, for exam-

ple. Philippe Ferret, who directs the experimental gardens of the magazine *L'Ami des jardins,* recommends the use not only of annuals but even perennials throughout the garden, especially those, like chrysanthemums or asters, that often need dividing and can be moved easily any time of year for seasonal color.

The danger, of course, is that the flowering plant may overpower nearby vegetables. One gardener who loves wild poppies finally had to resign herself to removing them from the vegetable garden, where they happily reappeared more plentifully from year to year, and proved so voracious that they stifled everything nearby. Many farmers make the same complaint: Encouraged not to use herbicides, and faced with tourists who love fields full of poppies, they protest that the wheat goes under while the flowers bloom.

To some extent indeed, emplacement depends on which flowers are being used, how easily they can be moved if necessary, and how likely they are to spread. Proliferation can vary tremendously from one climate and soil to another. Gardening books often describe a plant as invasive for one region that elsewhere must be coaxed into fragile growth. One person's weed is another person's treasure. Nowhere is this truer than for the flowers that thrive in a vegetable garden. Feverfew is but one example: This upright chamomile with golden green foliage and the typical daisy flowers of the family runs rampant in some

gardens, while at some plant fairs it is sold as a rare find. Any gardener wanting to add self-sowing and semiwild flowers to a vegetable plot should study carefully the local flora.

It is interesting to note that almost all of the flowers recommended today for vegetable gardens, whether for beauty or practical benefits or both, were grown in the early-seventeenth-century garden of Olivier de Serres. This early agronomist, one of the first to experiment with companion plantings, introduced many new varieties of both flowers and vegetables in his garden at Le Pradel, in the south-central Vivarais region. He produced a rich array of blooms for medicinal uses, for dyeing and other household purposes, as well as for sheer beauty. He made a distinction, however, between the vegetable plot and what he called "the pleasure garden." Pondering whether to put the flowers next to the house and in front of the vegetable plot, or on the contrary at the far end, beyond the potager, he wondered whether visitors would best enjoy an immediate dazzling display, or would prefer a gradual transition to brightest color—just as merchants show rich stuffs to their customers only after the coarser materials. Certainly the choice between immediate or overall effect and gently prepared surprise is still with us today.

Many experts recommend keeping a corner at one end of the potager for cut flowers. But, as one writer points out, this is also usually the nursery space, which soon produces so many seedlings that it is easy to distribute the overflow among the vegetables themselves or along the borders as the season progresses.

FLORAL BENEFITS

The choice of emplacement will depend not only on the visual effect desired but also on the practical aims pursued. A wide range of benefits is attributed to flowers in the vegetable garden: A certain variety of flower may stimulate the growth of nearby vegetables—pot marigolds (*Calendula*) next to tomatoes, for example. A line of lupins among the salads is recommended for providing light shade and extra nitrogen in the soil. Other flowers are reputed to protect neighbors against a variety of pests and diseases—marigolds (*Tagetes*) discourage nematodes in the soil. Some flowers draw beneficial insects, not only pollinating visitors like bees, but also ladybugs, hoverflies, lacewings, and other predators that can make short work of noxious aphids. Still other flowering plants, such as phacelia, are beneficial because they have deep roots that loosen the soil around them. Others act as climate indicators: cucurbits may be sown or set out when mock orange (*Philadelphus*) is in flower, tomatoes when hawthorn blooms, and corn when apple blossoms are falling. Flowering plants that are useful in preparing protective and nutritious sprays for vegetables include comfrey, tansy, and absinthe.

❧ *OPPOSITE TOP:* **Some gardeners so appreciate marigolds that the flowers not only accompany but dominate the composition—here with nasturiums and white cosmos in the farmyard Garden at Chaumont.**
❧ *OPPOSITE:* **Staked tomatoes are protected by companion plants 'Disco Orange' marigolds and 'Lea' chives. At the same time, they are interplanted with salad greens in an economical as well as decorative use of space.**

Then again, flowers may be grown that are edible in their own right—or drinkable, in the form of infusions or teas. Jasmine, orange, and acacia blossoms are eaten in some places, often as fritters. Bergamots (*Monardes didyma*) are not commonly regarded as edibles but their purple blossoms make good jellies and infusions.

If intended to protect or stimulate their neighbors, flowers must be placed right next to the target plant. The list of associations recommended to French gardeners is long and similar to those published in Holland, England, Germany, and America. A selection may be found in the general list of companion plants on page 177. Many gardeners swear by these. Others remain skeptical. A case in point is the wonderfully decorative spurge *Euphorbia lathyrus*, prized for its foliage more than for its flowers but reputed to repel moles. In some gardens, this effect is dramatic, in others nonexistent. Either it is a question of soil and climate affecting the composition of the plant's powerful sap, or some moles are smarter than others. However this may be, some gardeners will want to grow this plant for its strongly architectural character and willingness to self-sow. All should be careful to keep it away from young children; for if its juices affect moles, they are also said to be toxic to the muscle structure of human beings if absorbed into the system.

Four flowers are cited over and over again for multiple practical benefits, and all four also add bright, long-season color to the garden: pot marigolds, marigolds, borage, and nasturtiums.

Calendula (pot marigold) is credited with deterring beetles among asparagus and working against nematodes among carrots, tomatoes, and beets. Its petals can be used as a substitute for saffron in rice, or as a garnish for soups.

Tagetes (marigolds of the old-fashioned, strongly scented varieties) are said to ward off nematodes and to stimulate the growth of beans, cucumber, eggplant, melons, potatoes, pumpkins, and tomatoes.

Borago officinalis (borage) improves the flavor of cucurbits and tomatoes, increases the disease resistance of strawberries, and protects cabbage plants from common pests. Its roots loosen the soil. Its intense blue flowers add color to salads. Borage may become spindly by midsummer, but it can be cut back to grow again.

❧ *Top:* **Marigolds are certainly the most popular potager flower, providing reliable bloom all season long and, it is claimed, protection against nematodes in the soil.**
❧ *Above:* **Borage has everything: intense, purple-blue edible flowers, an inimitable growth habit, and valuable properties as a companion plant. And it self-sows.**

Tropaeolum majus (nasturtium), set among cabbage-family plants, celery, and cucumbers, is said to deter beetles and aphids and to improve the flavor of cucumber, radishes, and zucchini. Nasturtiums in pre-Columbian America were grown as food, and today the flowers add bright color and peppery flavor to mixed salads. The buds, picked just before opening, can be preserved in vinegar and used instead of capers. The pungent oil of nasturtiums (which are related to mustard) may draw cabbage moths and trick them into laying their eggs here rather than on nearby vegetables.

There is a great debate about nasturtiums and aphids: Do the flowers afford protection? Some experts say only against woolly aphids, whereas they are known on the contrary to attract the black ones. For this very reason, others consider nasturtiums valuable as decoy plants. Philippe Ferret recommends mixing them with artichokes . . . but perhaps largely for decorative reasons?

In any event, whereas pot marigolds, marigolds, and borage thrive in southern climates, nasturtiums usually fade away in intense heat, so they should not be relied on near the Mediterranean after June.

❧ When chef Jean Bardet sends out his kitchen staff with a list of herbs to pick, a typical harvest basket will contain chives, salad burnet, chervil, rosemary, basil, coriander, dill, parsley, arugula, sage, and marjoram—the whole topped off with colorful nasturtium blossoms.

FLOWERING VEGETABLES

Some vegetables themselves flower beautifully: The squash family has its bright yellow-orange trumpets among luxuriant green foliage, and zucchini blossoms, either by themselves or attached to tiny fruit, stuffed or fried, now count among the clichés of southern French restaurant cuisine.

Jerusalem artichokes produce tall spikes of daisies late in the season. The white tubercules have egg-yolk-colored flowers, but the rarer red roots produce a more orangey blossom and higher yields. Older French vegetable gardeners often shun these tubers, which stir memories of a severely restricted diet during World War II. Other gardeners appreciate their flavor, which has been likened to artichokes, lettuce, and even hazelnuts. It is claimed, moreover, that they are low in calories and high in iron, B vitamins, and fiber. Whether planted for food or decoration, Jerusalem artichokes should be regarded as a permanent plantation for at least five or six years.

The little-known, tender annual called shiso (*Perilla frutescens* 'Crispa') grows 2 to 3 feet high and bears spikes of lavender or pink flowers in fall, though it is grown mostly for its reddish purple fragrant foliage. Used as a seasoning, the latter's flavor has been compared with both mint and cinnamon. Its flower clusters are commonly used in Asian cuisine as fritters.

Many vegetables usually eaten before flowering are highly decorative if allowed to flower, whether planted especially for this purpose or because the crop supplies more than is needed for food. Any member of the cabbage family will produce huge bouquets of yellow blossoms very attractive to bees, often in late autumn or, in southern climates, in winter—most effective next to purple chard and the steely blue stalks of leeks. A few plants of almost any nonhybrid lettuce variety may be allowed to flower and self-sow; chicory in particular produces wonderfully intense blue blossoms that close around noon. Artichokes already have striking foliage, but may also be allowed to produce giant purple thistles. Onions and leeks left to go to seed make very beautiful large white or purple globes composed of small florets, and a few can be left on purpose for this reason. Chef Marc Meneau uses tiny leek buds as a seasoning in vegetable dishes.

❧ *Above & Opposite:* **Everyone loves a zucchini flower, from the bees that pollinate it to the cook who carefully stuffs it for steaming or deep-frying, to the photographer who delights in every stage of its opening. But the vegetable, smooth or rough, green or yellow, dark or speckled, is also quite beautiful.**

❧ *Below:* **Onions, leeks, and chives also offer beautiful globes of tiny blossoms, though usually only chives are allowed to flower.**

Saffron is a special case: *Crocus sativa*, which looks like any purple crocus but is fall-flowering, is grown for its pistils. According to myth, its warm yellow color was used by the gods of ancient Greece for their robes, as it is used even now by Buddhist monks. The Romans brought saffron from the East, and the Arabs introduced it into Spain, which was called by medieval Arab geographers "the land of saffron." In France, it used to be grown as a commercial crop not only in the south, where it is an essential ingredient of the famous fish stew *bouillabaisse*, but in the fourteenth century, it was grown also in the Gâtinais, north of Orléans. About fifty thousand flowers are required to produce a pound of saffron.

Easily cultivated by the home gardener, saffron likes poor, well-drained soil and is hardy to about 6° F., though it prefers hot summers. It can be planted in late July about 8 inches deep, at 3-inch intervals. The spot should be marked carefully since the leaves die back in March, as with other autumn crocuses, and the plants will be invisible until October. It flowers over a twenty-day period, and the pistils should be picked every morning, then dried in shade on absorbent paper in a very low oven. The bulbs should be replanted every two years.

BEAUTIFUL BLENDS

Karin Mundt writes regularly about flowers intermingled with vegetables in the magazine *Les Quatre saisons,* which has a big following among French organic gardeners. She generally recommends simple and well-known mixtures, easily acquired anywhere, which she appreciates for their beauty, fragrance, and beneficial influences. Violets, snowdrops, narcissus, and hyacinth start off the year in her garden, followed by wallflowers and madonna lilies which she blends with blue delphiniums, marigolds, pot marigolds, and chrysanthemums. She turns rueful at the sight of her vegetables, originally planted in orderly rows, half submerged at midseason by clumps of borage, poppies, pot marigolds, and nasturtiums (which can be very invasive in the Parisian climate, she warns). But these flowers contribute to the family's salads, and if they outstep their limits, they are easily pulled out and added to the mulch around taller vegetables. And the bees love all of them, so much so that visitors inquire if she has a hive nearby (she doesn't!).

Around Mundt's house grow other fragrant, bee-drawing plants: honeysuckle, honey locust (*Robinia acacia*), lime (linden) trees, old roses such as the *rose de Provins* or the rugosa with its particularly large hips, or the centifolia for fragrance.

Philippe Ferret, in his experimental gardens in Normandy, has a very different approach, based on meticulous study over several years of beautiful combinations of vegetables, flowers, and fruit. The aim, as he explains in the columns of *L'Ami des jardins,* is first and foremost decorative, not utilitarian. Ferret composes a great variety of pictures throughout the season. Among the easily moved perennials he recommends are lupins, daisies, and phlox. Room can be made for them by sowing vegetables with a bit more space between the rows and leaving room at the ends of rows. Dahlias, he feels, particularly benefit from rich potager soil; but Ferret also likes the tall silhouettes of gladioli, giant snapdragons, zinnias, and cleomes.

Here are some of his favorite combinations. They should work in any temperate climate on good soil.

🦗 Dahlias are another flower long accustomed to the company of vegetables in French potagers, and providing a seemingly unending variety of size, flower shape and color. Here seen at the Château de Galleville.

🦗 Rows (back to front) of orange cosmos (*Cosmos sulphureus* 'Flash'), staked and carefully pruned tomatoes, red cabbage, rudbeckia 'Marmelade' mixed with red impatiens and yellow marigolds, angelicas, and leaf chard.

🦗 For borders: dwarf nasturtiums, pinks, California poppies, white alyssum, ice plants, and portulaca. In particular, a mixture of red basil with dwarf nasturtiums and white alyssum.

🦗 Among artichokes: white and pink cosmos. Or, for an all-gray-toned composition, lavender, sage, verbascum, and horehound. Small-scaled climbers can be threaded among artichoke leaves: *Thunbergia alata,* climbing nasturtiums, or *Ipomoea quamoclit.* Another artichoke plot features double snapdragons 'Miss

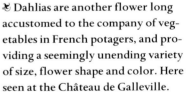

Butterfly', annual poppies, and a few red sages. It should be kept in mind that the artichoke's fountain of rough-toothed silver leaves may well disappear completely in the summer, or at least look tatty, and needs to be screened by something tall, like cosmos or climbing plants.

- In asparagus beds, Ferret recommends hollyhocks and cosmos.
- Carrots can be grown in rows flanked by orange cosmos and marigolds, not too close to avoid shading the carrots.
- Gold-leafed celery looks good with dwarf nasturtiums and kochias that take on flaming color in the fall.
- Cabbages can be grouped in squares with zinnias or chrysanthemums, and backed by a line of feathery fennel.
- Tall cabbage-family plants like brussels sprouts are set off with asters (Ferret loves *Aster datschii*). He recommends letting some old brussels sprouts stocks remain in place to flower in spring.
- Pattypan squash are prettier, he feels, than zucchini, especially the orange ones, mixed with annual hollyhocks, zinnias, blue sages, and dwarf sunflowers.
- Dwarf beans grow so fast that they present problems for season-long decor, but the red ones, 'Royal Burgundy', mix well with pink petunias, 'Rose du ciel'.
- Onions, garlic, and leeks that will overwinter are treated like any spring-flowering bulbs, and get a soft cover of *Viola cornuta*, wallflowers, silene, and forget-me-nots.
- Around pepper plants, Ferret suggests other sun-loving flowers like creeping verbenas, dwarf zinnias, and California poppies.
- Among tomatoes, spaced 2 feet apart: purple basil, borage, salpiglossis (painted tongue), rudbeckias, and perennial phlox.
- A carpet of New Zealand spinach can spread around hot pepper plants or be punctuated by tall marigolds here and there.
- Finally, under fruit cordons, Ferret likes lines of begonias and lettuce.

Obviously, all these combinations will require soil in top condition and copious watering, but any one of them would be delightful.

Top: The white and green foliage of the annual spurge, *Euphorbia marginata*, sets off brighter colors to good effect as here in the autumn garden at the Château de Saint-Jean-de-Beauregard.

Above: Pinks and carnations count among the most adaptable and decorative flowers to edge a vegetable bed, here in the company of a very low trained apple cordon, in the romantic garden of Wy-dit-Joli-Village.

Opposite: Effective combinations can result from the most commonplace elements: the soft greens of white-ribbed chard next to the blue daisy flowers of chicory allowed to bloom.

 In grand château potagers like Villandry, bedding plants like petunias and ageratum are still used to underscore the lines of dwarf box, creating particularly stong patterns when viewed from the terraces above.

Ornamental versions of commonly grown vegetables fit naturally into a potager: the great range of ornamental garlics, for example. Some actually smell of honey, like *Allium schuberti*. Spencer sweet peas are recommended as being the prettiest and most fragrant, but even the wild sweet pea, which will self-sow anywhere, can add its contribution of mauve-pink flowers in unexpected places.

At the famous potager of the Château de Villandry, each square is surrounded by flowers: daisies and pansies for spring, scarlet sage and hybrid verbena in summer and fall. One vegetable per square is especially chosen for color contrast with the floral edger: the steely-toned leek 'Bleu de Solaise', golden or red-ribbed chard, red-leafed lettuces, and so on. This use of colorful bedding plants belongs to the château tradition and is repeated in many others, including the manor house La Massonnière near Le Mans, where both marigolds and begonias, back to back, run in long lines under fruit cordons.

Novelist Pierre Gascar grew in his *jardin de curé*, among the leeks, lettuce, and carrots, the entire spectrum of rustic flowers. Even a shortened version of his list takes the breath away: from achillea and aubretia to bluebells, columbines, monkshood, echinops, hellebores, hostas, helianthemums, heuchera, incarvillea, irises (long considered edible), semperviviums, saxifrage, and veronicas, as well as all of the flowers already mentioned. Indeed, all of these and many more look fine in or around the vegetable garden, if borage, marigolds and nasturtiums remain the star performers.

Landscaper Pascal Cribier, for his pattern of thirty-six squares at Limésy mixing shrubs, herbs, vegetables, and flowers, chose brilliant daylilies, sedum 'Autumn Joy', zinnias, chrysanthemums, and iris for color.

Agronomist Olivier de Serres in the seventeenth century also grew violets, lily of the valley, lilies, gladioli, anemones, peonies, and tulips, and used strawberries as a border for the cutting garden. One of his prize flowering plants he called the "white truffle," and he was among the very first to believe it was also good to eat. Indeed, in the hands of a good cook, he claimed it to be the equal of the black truffle. This plant later gained fame as the humble potato. Its flower was so admired in the eighteenth century that it appears over and over again in the painted motifs of elegant *faïence* and porcelain.

All lovers of flowers and vegetable mixes seem to prefer the brightest possible colors—marigold edgers are very popular. Both Serres and—three centuries later—Colette loved amaranths, "purple fox-tails swinging in the breeze." Colette also admired geraniums, digitalis, the brightest reds and pinks of roses, Maltese cross, kniphofia, and red Chinese lanterns: "The whole hot garden fed upon an intense yellow light, with red and violet tremors."

Pierre Gascar suggests that bright flowers may best attract bees and other useful insects. Today's fashions in flower gardening tend to shun such display as garish, and certainly the humble marigold, dahlia, and zinnia are often regarded as vulgar. Those inclined to judge hastily might remember van Gogh's pleasure at such "amazing color," or ponder John Keats's praise of the same:

> *Open afresh your round starry folds,*
> *Ye ardent marigolds.*
> *Dry up the moisture of your golden lids,*
> *For great Apollo bids*
> *That in these days your praises should be sung*
> *On many harps which he has lately strung.*

American garden writer Henry Mitchell deserves the last word, perhaps, with his comment: "Marigolds are bright and beautiful if, like cousins, you don't have too many of them at once."

Herbs & Aromatics

Herbs and aromatic plants so obviously combine practicality and beauty that this type of gardening is one of the oldest in existence. The herb garden was first of all the earliest pharmacy, precious for its collection of medicinal plants. In different parts of France today, abbey and monastery gardens have re-created versions of medieval herb gardens organized for health care—one of the most beautiful is at the Prieuré de Salagon in Provence. Other early medicinal gardens, including those established by various kings of France, have been transformed into famous botanical gardens, *jardins de plantes,* like those in Paris or Montpellier.

But there were other uses for herbs, even in medieval times: dyeing cloth, combating insects such as moths in cupboards, making up a potpourri to perfume a room, and so on. Herbs were added to food as preservatives in times before refrigeration; or they masked the unpleasant tang of spoiling food and, it was hoped, lessened ill effects, thanks to their disinfectant properties. Today this category of plants is defined primarily as those that serve to enhance flavors, rather than as vegetables in their own right. The line is not always easily drawn: In the case of fennel, for example, the seeds, stems, and leaves may be added to a wide range of dishes, while the bulbous root of the Florentine variety provides a delicious vegetable. Whatever the problems of definition, however, herbs and aromatics are the traditional companions to vegetables in the French potager, every bit as much as flowers and small fruit trees.

Olivier de Serres, in his historic southern French garden, gave much room to the *plantes de bonne senteur* (fragrant herbs). He took inspiration from the aromatic gardens of the Medical School in Montpellier, which he saw in 1598 and which are still very much worth a visit today. At his domain, Le Pradel, he went so far as to construct a mock mountain, a sort of rockery, to give his herbs more sunshine. But he also used herbs as decorative edgers: lavender, rosemary, marjoram, basil, thyme, rue, and . . . mandrake root, all clipped low so as not to hide the inner parts of the beds. At a time when France was torn by religious wars, visitors to Serres's garden remarked with astonishment on "this assembly of so many plants living harmoniously in happy union, although having such diverse and extravagant differences."

Serres grew thistles for their seeds, which, mixed with white wine, improved the memory; mallow and marshmallow family plants; three sorts of chamomile; horehound to be used against coughs and sore throats; birth-

❦ *ABOVE:* **Lavender is available in many tones of purple, pink, and white. It attracts bees, and here mixes decoratively with phlox and coreopsis. Its flowers have many household and even culinary uses.**
❦ *OPPOSITE:* **At the Priory of Salagon in Haute-Provence, all the herbs and vegetables are species that were used in the Middle Ages, beautifully arranged with the church tower behind. The red blooms are *Lychnis coronaria*.**

wort for regulating women's periods; hypericum and calla lilies; and tobacco, considered in those days to be a universal curative, in particular for burns and wounds, headache, and toothache, and as an insecticide in the garden. Its name, *l'herbe de tous les maux* (the plant of all evils), might be taken in a contrary sense today.

Herbs in French potagers today are used in three major ways: intermingled with the vegetables as companion plants, expected to strengthen and protect their neighbors; as edgers to help outline the plots and give structure to the garden; in separate spaces of their own, usually along one side of the potager, in a formal arrangement.

HERBS AS COMPANIONS

Many gardeners include herbs among the vegetables, where they are particularly helpful as companion plants. Their capacity to protect against a variety of insects and diseases and to stimulate growth is due to the intensity of the aromatic oils they contain, which are often strongly disinfectant. The claims variously made for their beneficial effects are often debated, however, and much may depend on soil and climate, where such factors as humidity may make a difference. Sunny, dry climates increase the potency, both of taste and smell, of many low-growing, evergreen, shrubby aromatics, such as thyme, rosemary, sage, and lavender. These plants survive intense heat and drought by producing needle-like or tough, leathery leaves that limit evaporation as much as possible, thus concentrating their oils. They may therefore have stronger effects as companion plants in the south than in mild, wet climates, just as they have more pungent flavor in cooking.

Here follows a summary of herbal companion plantings commonly proposed by various French experts, with a description of both their beneficial associations and their decorative range:

DILL (*Anethum graveolens*), an annual, is widely recommended among carrots against fly. Dill among lettuces is also said to discourage snails, and to help the carrots form hearts without going to seed. Sometimes happy garden blends resemble those found at the table: Thus dill is suggested near cucum-

❧ Medieval gardeners grew herbs for many different purposes but mostly medicinal, using roots, stems, foliage, or flowers. In this medieval-style herb garden, rue forms large blue clumps with yellow flowers just beginning to open.

bers, cabbage, or beets. Experts claim dill has more vitamins than either parsley or paprika.

In the south, FENNEL is used rather than dill, but it is a perennial. Bronze fennel (*Foeniculum vulgare* 'Bronze')—often reddish, in fact—makes striking vertical accents and good texture contrasts, and has the same flavor as the green. Both, however, can be invasive and hard to dig up once big. Dill and fennel are both upright umbellifers with a delicate structure and thread-like leaves, flowering yellow, but fennel can grow so strongly that it overpowers its companions.

Another annual umbellifer, CORIANDER or CILANTRO (*Coriandrum sativum*), is associated with Chinese and Mexican food in the United States, and with North African cooking in France where it is sometimes called Arab parsley. It too should be sown among carrots, and it is also thought to bring out the flavor of potatoes, beets, and cucumbers.

All these herbs belonging to the umbellifer family also make pretty additions to dried bouquets if allowed to flower. In the garden, they attract bees and provide light shade in summer for nearby vegetables like lettuce. In cooking, they aid digestion.

PARSLEY (*Petroselinum sativum*), also an umbellifer, is in fact a biennial. It is said to increase vigor in onions and tomatoes, but to subdue more fragile plants such as lettuce. Parsley is notoriously long in germinating. The old garden folklore says it goes to the devil and back first. Soaking seeds for forty-eight hours before sowing is often recommended. Flat-leafed or Italian parsley (*persil simple* in French) is considered best for flavor but it is much less compact and decorative than the curly varieties. The late-nineteenth-century treatise on vegetables by Parisian seed merchant M. Vilmorin-Andrieux lists many more varieties than are currently available today, including Neapolitan or celery-leafed parsley, and fern-leafed parsley, the latter looking particularly appealing in the illustration.

CHERVIL (*Anthriscus cerefolium*), a low-growing, annual umbellifer, also contains large amounts of vitamin C and is much loved by French chefs. It has very fine, delicate foliage, makes an easy filler, and will self-sow once established. It is supposed to protect lettuce against aphids, mildew, snails, and slugs and also to drive away ants.

BORAGE (*Borago officinalis*) and SUMMER SAVORY (*Satureja hortensis*) are said to protect young cabbage or kale against stinkbugs and flea beetles. Summer savory is an old favorite mixed among peas and beans against aphids. It grows to about 1½ feet and its stems sometimes take on a purplish tint as it matures. Leaf celery is recommended for protection against cabbage moth and can make a pretty green manure among members of the cabbage family.

BASIL (*Ocimum basilicum*) counts as one of the most popular decorative as well as culinary herbs, coming in numerous colors, leaf sizes, and flavors, so that some gardeners have entire collections. Large- and small-leafed varieties, dark red and green, are the most common, and the most fashionable in recent years has been 'Purple Ruffles'. Basil is said to keep mildew off cucurbits. The Vilmorin treatise lists ten varieties, including one anise-scented and one called East Indian or tree basil. Specialist catalogues today regularly offer five or six.

❧ *OPPOSITE* **Most northern vegetable gardens save space for dill, with its delicate umbels and fragrant, thread-like foliage. Southerners generally use fennel instead. Savory flourishes in the gardens of Marc Meneau. Salad burnet is less well known, but is reputed to add a cucumber-like flavor to salads of mixed greens.**
❧ *BELOW:* **Chives and thyme serve many purposes, providing highly decorative edgings for vegetable beds as well as basic kitchen condiments.**

GARLIC (*Allium sativum*) is highly recommended around lilies and roses and all plants susceptible to mildew such as potatoes and tomatoes, but not near beans. Both the red and the white varieties are much appreciated. Many gardeners believe that each garlic stem should be tied in a knot when the bulbs are swelling to help prevent the plants from going to seed, and a bed of garlic thus knotted has a striking appearance. Since it is usually har-

HERBS &
AROMATICS

vested in late June (the occasion of many local festivals), it makes a good early-season crop, freeing the ground for midsummer.

CHIVES (*Allium schoenoprasum*) are also reputed to be good with roses, against mildew, black spot, and insect pests. There is a particularly ornamental giant variety with pink balls of flowers. The tufts, however, are more vigorous if cut often and not allowed to flower. Chives seem to do better if grown as an edger rather than in a bed, and if regularly divided. Some people much appreciate also Chinese chives, with white, starry flowers and flat leaves.

THYME (*Thymus vulgaris*) is said to protect against cabbage moth, snails, and slugs. *Farigoule,* as it is called in Provence, can be cultivated anywhere in France, at low altitudes in the north. Bush thyme is usually less than a foot high, and shows its pink or white flowers on fine, silvery foliage. It grows best on limy soil. Creeping thyme (*Thymus serpyllum*), known as *serpolet* in French, prefers acid, stony soil, makes large mats, and falls nicely over walls. There are numerous varieties of thyme of different heights, with plain or variegated foliage and pink or white flowers. Creeping thymes are sometimes proposed for paths, but it should be remembered that they attract bees when in flower and that this could prove a hazard in walking.

The whole family of artemisias has beautiful silver foliage and pungent odors. It fell into disrepute in the late nineteenth century when one of its members, ABSINTHE or wormwood (*Artemisia absinthium*), was used to make an addictive drink that destroys nerve centers. Absinthe caused the downfall of many bohemian artists and writers, such as the poet Paul Verlaine. This potent family actively inhibits the growth of plants growing near it, is not good for soil, and even drives away earthworms. But it is reputed to protect gooseberries and black currants from rust.

WORMWOOD makes a well-branched bushy shrub of about 5 feet that needs cutting back several times a season. Southernwood (*A.abrotanum*) reaches about the same size and is a vigorous spreader. Roman wormwood (*A.pontica*) makes a beautiful matted ground cover that can never be removed without leaving a bit behind. *A.schmidtiana* is better behaved at 2 feet, and it also has a much appreciated dwarf form. The various varieties possess such delicate, feathery leaves that few gardeners resist having artemesias somewhere, but perhaps outside the vegetable plot.

A notable exception is TARRAGON (*Artemisia dracunculus*), a "must" in any herb garden though it should be cut back to avoid falling all over itself. It has a good, medium green color and slim leaves.

Common garden SAGE (*Salvia officinalis*) protects against cabbage moth, aphids, snails, and slugs. It has three main ornamental varieties: one purplish red, one yellow-flecked, and the third mixing white, red and green in its leaves. The yellow one (*Salvia officinalis* 'Icterina') is the sturdiest and most reliable; the other two sometimes die back unexpectedly, in part or in whole, and have to be replaced fast. All bear purple spikes of flowers in early summer and hang nicely over walls.

❧ *ABOVE:* **Fine-leafed thyme and tarragon set off the broad foliage of a grapevine in this garden near Lyons. Herbs provide many interesting texture contrasts in the decorative potager.**

Sage cuttings root easily, and the plants also sucker readily. It is said that he who grows sage in his garden will never need a doctor.

Less well known, HYSSOP (*Hyssopus officinalis*) has stunning, bright, blue-spiked flowers and small, narrow green leaves on an evergreen bush about a foot high. It is said to protect against cabbage moth, snails, and slugs. It can be used in cooking with beans, or in stuffings, and also for herb teas.

RUE (*Ruta graveolens* or "herb of grace") has a lovely blue-green color and texture, especially the variety 'Jackman's Blue'. There is also a variegated kind. And rue's yellow flowers contrast nicely with the foliage. But the plant's juices can burn the fingers and the smell is intense, not appreciated by all. It is recommended near roses, and should be trimmed right after flowering so that it will not get scraggly.

Although some annual herbs, particularly the basils, regularly find themselves used to outline a bed, it is most often the perennials, especially the woody or shrubby ones, that appeal for this purpose. These make, in effect, dwarf hedges. Of course it is easier to leave perennials in place from year to year on the edge rather than in the middle of a bed. Some of those listed for their beneficial qualities as companions also make good edgers: chives, thyme, hyssop, sage, among them. Winter savory is another good possibility. Lavender also nicely borders a vegetable plot. At the manor house garden of La Massonnière near Le Mans, four rectangular beds of vegetables are laid out around a stone-edged pool, and the inner corner of each bed, near the pool, has been rounded off and beautifully outlined with dwarf lavender 'Hidcote'.

Lavandula angustifolia, the most commonly found LAVENDER variety, also comes as 'Alba' and 'Rosea' with white or pink flowers. In acid soil *L. stoechas pedunculata* (French lavender) provides an attractive lower variety. It grows wild in Mediterranean France and is less hardy. There are several common dwarf cultivars of *L. angustifolia*, however: 'Hidcote', 'Nana Alba', 'Loddon Pink', and 'Munstead' among them. Lavender may be thought to have a purely decorative function, or a use only in sachets and perfumes, but today this herb is more and more frequently used to flavor desserts. The rich aroma of lavender honey has long been appreciated in Provence, after all, and now it appears often in ice cream and *crèmes brûlées*.

ROSEMARY (*Rosmarinus officinalis*), though not so hardy as lavender, does make a perennial bush all over France. The common, wild variety has pale blue flowers and in its native habitat can grow 5 feet tall and spread as much. But here too there are many varieties, some with white and pink flowers, others with draping or cascading rather than upright shapes. Rosemary takes a lot of room as an edger and should be kept for large spaces. It also makes a good plant for the top of sheltered walls. Rosemary blooms for a long period in winter when little else does. Care should be taken to get a long-flowering variety, that will add color from November to March, as they are not all the same.

GERMANDER (*Teucrium chamaedrys*) has pink-purple flowers in early summer on neat, evergreen, low-growing bushes. Often overlooked in the garden, it grows wild in many parts of southern France.

All of these aromatic edgers need to be cut back at least once in the season to create a neat line—treated, indeed, as low-growing hedges.

Chef Marc Meneau, at Vézelay, uses bush thyme in an original manner, not quite as an edger nor yet in a separate space. His squares of vegetables are each organized into four equal triangles around a tall central plant. In one bed, an entire triangle is filled permanently with bush thyme. The other

❧ *OPPOSITE:* **At La Massonnière, vegetables are spread out symmetrically around a central, stone-edged basin. The corner of each square near the junction has been rounded off and planted with a stripe of deep blue 'Hidcote' lavender.**

❧ *OVERLEAF:* **In Provence, herb gardens are not traditional because aromatics cover every hillside. But contemporary gardeners create very beautiful ones, here with box, santolina, and white-flowered lavender.**

three contain vegetables that change throughout the season. This is somewhat similar to landscape architect Pascal Cribier's intermingling of vegetables, flowers, shrubs, and herbs in a series of squares at Limésy. The contents of some parts evolve throughout the season, but a solid backbone is provided by evergreen shrubs and bushy aromatics that stay in place from year to year. Both designers have blended the herb and vegetable gardens into a single design in an original manner.

SEPARATE HERB GARDENS

Traditionally, however, aromatics occupied a space of their own—in château gardens, for example. The logic here is much the same as for any other permanent planting, such as bush fruit or asparagus, that would get in the way of digging for annual and semiannual crops if mixed in. But perhaps in the case of herbs, a separate section alongside the vegetable garden also allowed a better display of the elegant, formal compositions to which these plants lend themselves so beautifully.

Finally, a separate herb garden is often recommended because many aromatics have powerful and invasive roots, such as mint or oregano, or self-sow very readily, like bee balm; it is easier to contain them in their own domain.

In Mediterranean France, famous for its cooking herbs such as thyme, savory, sage, and rosemary, herb gardens are not traditional at all. In these regions, gardeners generally pick their herbs wild in the way that people go mushrooming elsewhere. Scrubby, limestone hillsides exposed to strong southern sun grow miles and miles of herbs far more pungent than the richer, regularly watered soil of any home garden could produce. Formerly, in such regions, gardeners saved their efforts for the herbs that need careful cultivation and water to thrive, like basil. Thus Colette Lafon, a follower of Gertrud Franck in the Alpes Maritimes, does not plant herbs in her garden as companion plants (except for coriander among carrots) because lavender, thyme, rosemary, and oregano grow on hillsides all around her. She gets much the same benefits, however, by picking branches of these aromatics and mixing them with bay leaves, nettles, cistus, myrtle and comfrey in her shredder, to produce a woody mulch that she then spreads between rows of vegetables.

❧ *ABOVE:* **The Lafourcade herb garden in Provence is a self-contained, intimate, beautifully designed space of small beds planted near a bench, where the visitor can sit and catch the rich scents on the air.**
❧ *OPPOSITE:* **Herbs lend themselves to planting in pots, which can be decoratively grouped outdoors in summer and brought into the kitchen in winter. Here thyme and basil in the garden of Bruno Goris.**

Today, despite tradition, many southerners design herb gardens for the sheer visual pleasure of the arrangements they allow. Aromatics are particularly versatile plants. But, perhaps because so many of them prefer a stony soil, formal patterns of herbs are generally set within a mineral framework. Landscaper Dominique Lafourcade uses a design with river pebbles in a circle. At the Château de Saint-Jean-de-Beauregard near Paris bricks outline the different sections allotted to different herbs along the base of a weathered old wall. Chef Jean Bardet of Tours plants his aromatics in lightly raised and mounded squares, cut into four by diagonal lines of rounded bricks.

Very often, herbs are planted in a kind of thematic mixed border, a long strip along one side of the garden with rather more formal design than is usual in purely decorative plantings. Emphasis here, however, is on the flowering aromatics intermingled with shrubs and country-garden flowers (indeed, blooms for cutting are also traditionally planted in such a strip). In this case, the same plants may be repeated at regular intervals: silver weeping pear trees and tall clumps of angelica in the large-scale herb border in a private garden in Provence; purple hazelnuts at

❧ Mint, sage, and variegated
periwinkle (*Vinca major*) strug-
gle for dominance in one bed of
this medieval herb garden, at
the foot of one of the owner's
own sculptures. For the
moment, the low box hedge
manages to contain them.

Saint-Jean-de-Beauregard (against a wall that encloses the
orchard, however, not really in the herb garden proper). In a
narrower, smaller-scaled strip at the Château d'Opme in the
Auvergne, alternating clumps of feverfew, catnip, achillea, and
perovskia create a white, blue, yellow and purple composition.

Nowhere in the potager is the tapestry effect more
telling than in the section devoted to herbs. Herb gardens
achieve their beauty from contrasts of foliage color and texture, highlighted
throughout the season by flowers here and there. But special attention should be

134

HERBS &
AROMATICS

given to their different heights, which can vary tremendously and make a big impact. Several herbs are striking, tall-standing plants, like fennel and angelica. Clary sage (*Salvia sclarea*) is another unusual and beautiful tall plant with large, woolly leaves and flower spikes that can vary from almost pure white to pink and blue mixed, changing as they age. Its fragrance is almost overpowering.

LOVAGE (*Levisticum officinale*) looks like a large celery plant, with a mound of leaves rising up to 3 feet, stalks up to 6 feet, and hollow stems that are used like celery. It needs freezing temperatures in winter and does not like hot summers.

SWEET CICELY (*Myrrhis odorata*) has tall, well-branched, ferny foliage making a plant over 3 feet high. Roots, stems, and young leaves can all be eaten. Added to fruit desserts, they lessen the amount of sugar needed.

CHERVIL ROOT (*Chaerophyllum bulbosum*, in French *cerfeuil tubéreux*) has known great popularity among French chefs in recent years for its delicately flavored roots. It can grow 6 feet high and has small white umbelliferous flowers; it is very hardy and likes moisture in the soil.

Among herbs of medium height (2 to 3 feet), the agastasche family has several decorative perennial members that find their way into French herb gardens. Also known as giant or MEXICAN HYSSOP, they have purple spikes and fresh, soft, indented foliage that can be chopped and added to salads. *Agastache foeniculum,* anise hyssop, grows about 2 feet tall and is hardier than *A.mexicana*.

HORSERADISH (*Armoracia rusticana*) makes a 2- to 3-foot-high clump of exotic-looking leaves. The roots are dug up once a year but can never be entirely removed. The flavor of the grated root is so strong that horseradish used to be called *moutarde de capucin* (monk's mustard).

MINT can be a menace and, to keep it from proliferating, many gardeners plant it in big pots, buried. But there are so many mint varieties—differing in height, shape, texture, and flavor—but all decorative, that there too, collectors have a field day.

FEVERFEW (*Chrysanthemum parthenium*) makes a 2- to 3-foot bush with daisy flowers and often sows itself happily all over the garden. *Matricaria recutita* syn. *chamomilla* has similar habits and its flowers make the best tea in the group of plants commonly called chamomile. The creeping one, an evergreen perennial that can be used as a groundcover, is called *Anthemis nobilis*. It spreads readily, has lovely small daisies and filigree foliage.

MARJORAM (*Marjorana hortensis*) and OREGANO (*Oregano vulgaris*), closely related to each other, grow to about 2 feet and come in several colors of foliage: reddish tinted, blue, yellow. In the latter, it is the new growth that is bright, fading to green in summer. These herbs with tracing, underground roots are harder to manage than the clearly shrubby ones, but for that reason they make good groundcovers in dry soil. Marjoram is annual in the north, perennial in the south, since it freezes at 18° F.

BEE BALM (*Melissa officinalis*) is a pretty plant whose foliage of soft indented leaves and small white flowers grows to about 2 feet. It easily gets scraggly on the one hand, and invasive on the other, but it makes good tea. Its leaves can be cut up for salads. There are golden and variegated bee balms as well.

Also low-growing (about 1 foot), salad burnet or pimprenelle (*Poterium sanguisorba* syn. *Sanguisorba minor*) makes a pretty blue-green rosette of pinnate leaves that can be added to salads. Marinated in vinegar, they add a cucumber-like flavor. It is partially evergreen. The flowers themselves are rather nondescript.

An important category of decorative aromatics is those that have showy flowers. A much-beloved and versatile family is the catnip group, from the tall, white-flowered, wild *Nepeta cataria,* to the creeping, purplish-blue *Nepeta x faassinii* and *N.mussinii,* and in particular the medium-sized cultivar 'Six Hill's Giant' that makes luxuriant clumps flowering over a long period and will flower again if cut back.

Tansy's yellow flowers (*Tanacetum vulgare*) make a nice foil for blue-flowered catnip. It looks much like yellow achillea with somewhat smaller clumps (2 to 3 feet) and is also good in dried arrangements. A vehement self-sower, it also cannot be moved without leaving some little bit of root that will resurrect relentlessly. Tansy leaves are used to make a spray for garden vegetables to control insect pests.

Perennial horsemint or Oswego tea (*Monarda didyma*) grows 2 to 3 feet high, and comes with deep red, purple, and blue flowers. Flax (*Linum*), the annual with red or the perennial with blue blossoms, was once an important textile plant. Nor should one forget the marigolds, pot marigolds, and borage already recommended for sowing among vegetables, and—not least—the garden iris, the root of which first drew attention to itself as an edible plant. Here the range of colors and sizes is immense.

As English poet Andrew Marvell put it in the seventeenth century: "How could such sweet and wholesome hours Be reckoned but with herbs and flowers?"

❦ At the Château de Saint-Jean-de-Beauregard, herbs grow among the vegetables, but there is also a separate space where bricks laid in the earth outline squares and triangles. These quickly disappear in season under the exuberant foliage.

❧ SEASONS

T ime and change are both the delight and bane of gardeners, but everyone enjoys the unfolding of the seasons. As the English writer William Cobbett put it in 1829, "to watch the progress of the crops is by no means unentertaining to any rational creature." The kitchen garden evolves faster than any other: The cycle of growth to maturity can take as little as eighteen days, in the case of the famous high-speed radishes. The gardener has to begin again constantly throughout the season. In decorative vegetable gardening, the greatest challenge is maintaining a harmonious picture all year round, taking into account the bare earth common at the time of sowing, which may appear again in even more irregular patches when vegetables are harvested. A row of red cabbage set against golden celery and bronze fennel will certainly please the eye, but when one cabbage turns into salad, will the result be like a smile with one front tooth missing? Even before harvesting, irregularities creep in: Inevitably two or three cabbages will grow less well than the other eight or nine. Even if the row remains perfect and highly photogenic, the space remains occupied over a long season by red cabbage that the family may eat only once a month at best, thus taking up room without providing food. As always, there must be compromises.

Although it is true that seasonal change is the most difficult aspect of decorative vegetable gardening to control, there are a number of helpful techniques. The first perhaps is for the gardener to learn to enjoy the irregularities of pattern that harvesting may produce as much as those that occur through the self-sowing of annuals and biennials—some of which indeed provide convenient fillers for gaps. No ornamental garden is perfect all the time. One consolation for unwelcome surprises is that time works for as well as against the gardener, and that bare patches will not remain empty for long.

SPRING

Spring comes at different times in different climates. The first step in planning, for both an ornamental and a productive garden, is to know local growing conditions. Climate will determine when the show can get under way, when it will reach its peak, and when it will settle into gentle but elegant decline. And climate dictates what possibilities exist for winter beauty.

❧ *ABOVE:* **Each season has its beauty, even in the vegetable garden, where cabbage family plants in particular may withstand heavy frosts in a most decorative manner.**
❧ *OPPOSITE:* **Six months later, young cabbage plants are tender and green while carrots are ready for the table. By now it may be necessary to water daily.**

France usually is described as having five climate zones: the oceanic, extending from the north along the Atlantic coast south to the Pyrenees; the "transitional," extending outward around Paris; the continental, covering the northeast corner of Alsace-Lorraine; the mountain climate of the Jura and Alps, the Pyrenees, and parts of the center; and finally the Mediterranean, in Provence, on the Riviera, and in Corsica—wherever olive trees can survive. Each of these zones, of course, contains many local variations and differences.

French gardening guides usually fix growing seasons with respect to the Parisian norm, in numbers of days more or less. For example, if an apple variety matures on September 15 in Paris, it may be ready a month earlier in the south, two weeks later in the north or in the mountains.

France thus possesses a tremendous diversity of local conditions in an area smaller than Texas. The beautiful contrasts of its landscapes, from region to region, suggest what variety can be found in its gardens. Then, too, there are the yearly fluctuations, the subject of endless conversations among gardeners everywhere, who are always bemused by the current season's advance or delay with respect to a mythical norm. And what of the phenomenon of microclimates, which can create many surprises even within a single garden? One southern gardener recounts that her peach trees regularly flower at the same time as her almond trees, which is not at all according to normal expectation, but results from the former enjoying a particularly sheltered position denied the latter.

Inevitably, vegetable gardens get under way much later north of the Loire than in the Midi. In 1994, Philippe Ferret proposed to the readers of the popular magazine *L'Ami des jardins* two models for beginning gardeners: two plots, the first about 20 feet square, the other about 30. These were photographed first in June, when the first sowings and plantings were made in bare earth, then in August, when a pleasing pattern of varied textures had become established, then in September when the runner beans had climbed to the top of their supports, the marigold borders had tripled in volume and flowered brilliantly, and rows of bronze fennel and corn had begun making their presence felt. A number of lettuce plants had by then gone to seed, including red-leafed ones, and were left

❧ Southern gardens, like the Riviera potager of Bruno Goris, supply vegetables all year round and may be at their least attractive in the dry, hot month of August when northern potagers are luxuriant.

in place. By fall, therefore, the tapestry took on a third dimension and considerable color, while the harvest basket filled up fast.

In the south, this timetable would be unthinkable, even for a new garden. Spring comes much earlier. Garlic, broad beans, and peas are sown before Christmas. The last killing frost (in a "normal year") may be in March or April. No one could imagine having bare earth in June—unless as a result of digging up the first potato crop. Of course, many northern gardens are already under way by June when not in their first year, as in Ferret's examples. But most are not well filled in until July, unless they benefit from extensive greenhouse reserves.

Northern potagers can be beautiful in spring, however. Château gardens in Normandy, for example, owe much of their spring beauty to the flowering of apple and pear cordons that surround the still-bare plots, often seconded by huge clumps of narcissus, peonies, and roses, which may be generations old. Even smaller gardens can take a tip from this tradition, and frame the vegetable plot with spring-flowering bulbs, perennials, and fruit trees to provide color at a time when vegetable seedlings still hardly show.

In the south, no gardener would dream of starting up a new garden as late as June because all efforts would be doomed by summer heat and drought. Northerners moving south and beginning to garden are often completely overwhelmed by the pace. Cecilia Phillips, a Scotswoman who moved to Provence in the 1960's, recorded her amazement at picking plums in the second week in June. She noted that her spinach regularly bolted by then no matter how much it was watered, and that it

was useless to sow peas after the end of April. They could, however, be started again in late August and early September along with a new planting of early-ripening potatoes, a kind of second spring.

At the Château de Villandry in the Loire Valley, always the great model for French decorative vegetable gardening, two definite seasons are scheduled yearly. First, in late March, after the last heavy frosts, gardeners sow or set out peas, broad beans, lentils, romaine lettuce, cut-and-come-again oak-leaf lettuces, and turnips. In June, there is a massive change of scene, when some 140,000 plants from the greenhouse are used to create the famous patterns of the great parterre: eggplant, peppers, regular and cherry tomatoes, carrots, Turk's-head squash, gourds, endive, horseradish, red cabbage, basil, blond white-ribbed chard and rhubarb chard, golden celery, corn salad, red beets, parsley, blue leeks, and ornamental cabbages. Seeds are used also: tomatoes already sizable will be oversown with different colors of lettuce, for example. In November, the major harvest takes place, and the produce is sold in the village. Only leeks remain in the ground at Villandry all winter.

SUMMER

"Summer afternoon—summer afternoon; to me those have always been the two most beautiful words in the English language." Thus wrote Henry James. (Gertrude Stein was later to prefer the sound of "cellar door," more original perhaps but less inspiring.) Though the phrasing of "summer afternoon" is heavier in French, many continental gardeners would share James's sentiment. Vegetable gardens especially are at their best in midsummer, when the beds have filled in nicely but the lines are still clearly visible. "Midsummer," however, means rather different experiences between north and south. By the Mediterranean, no one would think of gardening in the heat of the day. Siesta is far more appropriate for summer afternoons, before or after a swim. Summer gardens in the south require hours of watering, and this takes place most effectively before nine in the morning or at after six at night—when the light is also soft and colors vibrant, and the garden particularly beautiful.

Nonetheless, in all climates growers of decorative vegetable gardens are faced with the problem of midsummer holes after harvest. Edging plants around plots can mask these gaps to some extent. Or one can plan a dramatic focal point, a stand of amaranths, for example, in the middistance beyond an early-maturing crop like new potatoes, so that the eye will be drawn over the hole. The best solutions, however, seem to be fast-growing fillers and stopgap plants, including the invaluable green manures. Or, if living material is not available, some sort

of mulch that is good-looking, easily moved, and effective against weeds and drought.

Green manures and mulches certainly help any vegetable garden in a number of ways, and can prove particularly useful when seeking decorative effect. In France as elsewhere there is much interest in green manures. Their practical benefits are numerous: Strong roots break up the soil, some add nitrogen, or draw out minerals that are thus made available for following crops; they grow fast and suppress weeds, while some such as rye and buckwheat cleanse the soil and can protect it from runoff in heavy rains. Cut and allowed to dry, green manures produce a thick mass of mulch or compost.

Many French gardeners, whether decorative or just practical, swear by mustard. It sows well in difficult conditions, grows fast as a filler plant, has a bright, cheerful green foliage and yellow or white flowers if allowed to remain long enough, produces a good volume of plant material, and decomposes fast. Considered a deterrent to slugs, and recommended at the foot of tomato plants if kept no more than hand high, it also is said to disinfect the soil. In most parts of France, although not the south, it is killed by winter frosts, so is never invasive. In any case, mustard can easily be pulled up or dug in, unlike some of the tougher alternatives.

Clovers seem to be more controversial, in spite of their property of enriching the soil with nitrogen. Annual kinds sown in early March produce pretty foliage and prepare the ground for summer plantings. Experts recommend digging in clover only eight days in advance of planting, but this will work only in a moist climate where decomposition takes place fast. Some French vintners now underplant their vines with a white-flowering variety of clover that is very pretty in midsummer. Other kinds can also be sown in later summer as a fall green manure crop, and they help keep the garden green until killed back by hard frost. Violet clover overwinters and prepares the ground for late-spring plantings. The danger with clover is in choosing varieties that become pests—hard to get rid of once their usefulness is over.

The absolute king of green manures for the decorative garden is phacelia, sometimes called in English "bee's friend," with good reason. There are two varieties currently available: *P. tanacetifolia* and *P. campanularia,* the first with soft violet-blue feathery flowers, and the second with deep blue bells. A leguminous plant, phacelia also enriches the soil with nitrogen, and is not only a quick filler but a lovely flowering

❧ *Phacelia tanacetifolia,* the "bee's friend," is fast becoming the most popular green manure crop for decorative gardening because it enriches the soil, is easy to handle, and has flowers of such a lovely color.

plant over a long season. *Phacelia tanacetifo-lia* is not, however, neat-looking in small spaces, getting leggy very fast. In some regions, French farmers have begun to grow it in fallow fields, creating dazzling accents in the landscape, with much the

🌿 The first frost withers the cherry tomatoes, but spares the marigolds temporarily. Tender salads thrive under the protection of a glass bell. Today, plastic domes and fiber films are more common in home gardens, far more practical but less aesthetic.

same effect as mustard, rapeseed, or poppies in flower elsewhere.

Quite a few other flowering plants not generally used as green manures have shown themselves useful for stopping the gaps caused by harvesting in a dec-orative potager. A small nursery near the cutting garden is invaluable as a source of cosmos or pot marigolds that can be transplanted to the needed spot to hide the soil virtually overnight. Failing that, many gardeners simply allow such plants to self-sow. As they weed from month to month, they come upon these small treasures already growing in odd corners, ready to move where they will. Borage, larkspur, love-in-a-mist, clary sage, and many more (see list of self-sowers page 175) can all be used thus. Sweet alyssum is useful as a filler as well as for edg-ing, but various types and colors of lettuce, often readily available as transplants at the local market, are perhaps one of the easiest solutions and one that will not drain the soil too much.

Cover cropping—the sowing of two crops together that will mature at different rates—is another essential technique to master. The mixing of radish seed with carrots is often cited as the best example, the radishes germinating quickly so that the line of carrots is clearly visible and hence not disturbed. From an aesthetic point of view, the radishes serve to mask bare earth until the froth of young carrot foliage emerges. The radishes will of course be harvested at a time when the carrots are still tiny.

❧ Straw makes a good mulch among strawberry plants, keeping ripening fruit off damp ground. Many gardeners, however, find pine needles more aesthetic, and their acidity is readily tolerated by strawberries.

In the *Lazy Man's Beautiful Garden* authors Beucher and Collaert recommend, for example, keeping one section of the potager each year for plants of the Liliaceae family: onions and their cousins. Early on, they set out onion bulb sets in rows, separated by a strip of mustard that can be walked on when necessary (so they say, but it should be done carefully) and dug under in May. In July, when the onions are nearly ripe, leeks will be planted where the mustard was.

Squashes, which make a wonderful sea of wavy green foliage around brightly colored fruit by the end of the season, take a while to get started, and can certainly benefit from a noncompetitive underplanting. Besides those plants reputed to help their growth (like borage and nasturtiums), lettuce, radishes, and spring onions can be grown among the squashes, or any other low-growing annual flower that will be at its best in spring and early summer. Or if the gardener prefers not to use a lot of space on cucurbits and to risk bald patches early in season, he or she can imitate the French chefs Jean Bardet and Marc Meneau, and grow squash on a special trellis, or picket fence, or in pots along the top of a wall.

Renewing the pattern of a decorative vegetable garden gets most challenging in the height of summer, when the ground may harden in spite of watering, nature's supply of plantlets dries up along, thankfully, with the weeds, and harvesting is already in full swing. At this point mulching may be the best solution both for the garden's well-being and for aesthetic reasons. Choices of mulch are more limited when appearances count, of course: Black plastic will offend the eye, even bright fresh straw may be found a bit glaring (as well as greedy for nitrogen in the soil). Decomposing vegetable matter, as in the Franck method (a kind of sheet composting), may be acceptable when the vegetables are big enough to hide the surface between them, or if the spaces are lightly covered with something more appealing, such as dry straw or grass clippings that have already turned sere. One old gardener uses a mature mix of manure and barley straw that looks very good and does wonders for the garden. Flat stones or earthenware tiles can be helpful in special cases, as under the ripening fruit of melons and squash to keep the fruit from contact with wet earth. More permanent plantings allow for a wider choice again, and certainly strawberries, with their love of acid soil, do well with a neat and highly presentable pine needle mulch. Pine bark is also now widely available in France as in the United States.

Suitable covers must also be found to keep summer sowings moist, especially of crops hard to germinate, like mâche, which every French vegetable gardener

wants for the fall or winter garden. One good-looking summer mulch for this purpose is dried fern fronds, which can be convenient if there are stands nearby. These have a soft rust tone and decompose slowly without help, enriching the soil. Other gardeners shade summer sowings with *canisse,* cheap and readily available reed fencing that can be cut to size and laid over a frame. A natural material the color of old straw, it looks good though it is not long-lasting, and must be removed for watering.

Some gardeners cover summer sowings with textile films meant for that purpose, but even those tinted green are not beautiful. An unusual solution was discovered by a manufacturer of sisal mats traditionally used in the pressing of olives. After severe frosts in 1956 killed many olive trees, this company, based in Nyons, in Provence, had to diversify its production, but it kept to coconut fiber as its main resource. It now manufactures (among many other things) rolls of sisal netting for use on slopes to hold new plantings. But the netting also makes an excellent and discreet cover for new sowings in hot weather. Laid gently on the ground after sowing and watering, the webs keep in moisture; they can be delicately removed when seedlings have sprouted but are still very small.

It is always best to check local resources for mulching, and then consider the pros and cons of each: Is

❧ *Top:* **Many materials can be used to cover summer sowings and keep in moisture in hot weather while not stifling young plants. Here netting made from coconut fiber has been laid down, next to last winter's leeks gone to seed.**

❧ *Above:* **A French proverb says that a gardener is as good as his melons. To help maturing melons ripen without rotting, many support each fruit with terracotta tiles either laid flat or standing upright in the sea of foliage.**

the sawdust too fresh? What wood does it come from? Will it look cakey and unpleasant, or can it be covered lightly with something more sightly? Is seaweed readily available? What will it look like a month from now? Many new commercial mulches have recently become available that contrive to be both practical and pleasing, for both short- and long-term use. If they prove expensive, the thrifty gardener can use them to mask a layer of decomposing spinach or mustard underneath.

A light mulch in summer will also hide drip irrigation systems, but it must not be so dense as to prevent their efficient operation. It might be thought that southern gardens could best profit from mechanized irrigation, and of course today many do. But the traditional method of watering in these regions requires bare earth between plants. It is quite elegant though tricky to command. It involves designing with a hoe—early in the season when the soil is not yet hard—a series of shallow canals throughout the garden that will lead water along each row when the hose is turned on, or the valve opened from a larger canal (often part of the public irrigation network) along the garden's edge. Water flows gently through this intricate, miniature canal system to the foot of each waiting plant.

Lady Fortescue, describing her garden near Nice in the 1950's, records a particularly dramatic version of this age-old technique. The water was stored in a big reservoir, a great, stone tank at the top of the steep, terraced hillside, from which it descended in channels of cement. To start the operation, the gardener Hilaire took out a huge plug. The water cascaded down, Hilaire rushing in pursuit as it overflowed its banks down toward the shallow trenches dug between lines of tomatoes and lettuce. When each channel was a miniature stream, Hilaire feverishly raked the soil at its end into a little dam to close it, so that the water permeated gently to the roots of the plants. "It is a thrilling game," wrote Lady Fortescue from the sidelines, "as he has to be very quick. . . ." In August, this feat took place at 5:30 A.M. But if Hilaire saw a snail cross his path with only one horn extended, he knew rain was on the way and refrained from watering.

Today's organic gardeners sometimes recommend upending a plastic bottle with its bottom cut off at the roots of large plants like tomatoes and zucchini, to be filled from the hose for slow, deep watering at the roots. Decorative gardeners must shun this solution; but a more aesthetic version can be provided by terra-cotta flower pots buried next to each plant when it is first set out. The hole should be almost completely blocked with a pebble, then the pot can be filled once a day during hot weather. This method also has the advantage of allowing fairly exact measurements of the water used. Experts claim it takes some twenty gallons of water to produce one pound of lettuce. An old French proverb reminds us, however, that one good hoeing is worth two waterings (*Un binage vaut deux arrosages*).

In some cases, flavor if not looks will improve with less watering. This is one of the main differences between commercially grown tomatoes and peaches at the height of summer and those produced by the home gardener without industrial irrigation. The latter remain smaller, perhaps, but have incomparable taste. Alice B. Toklas remarked that the gooseberries of the upper garden in Bilignin, the one that remained unwatered, often had much more intense flavor than those grown near the spring. This may be a consolation to the many city dwellers who see their potagers only on weekends.

AUTUMN

French poet Francis Ponge considers that plants express time in terms of space, by the room "they occupy little by little, filling in a design no doubt predetermined forever. When they have finished this task, a certain weariness overtakes them. And this is the drama of yet another season."

By autumn, the potager is full to overflowing, and it is much easier to harvest without leaving holes in the design. Plants like corn and Jerusalem artichoke are satisfyingly tall. Expansive plants like squash have filled in, tomato garlands are hung with vibrant fruit. If drought and disease have been kept at bay, autumn is indeed the time, in the words of John Keats, "of mellow fruitfulness, close bosom-friend of the maturing sun." Not much need be done at this stage to improve the garden's beauty except harvesting and tidying. Dahlias, chrysanthemums, asters, and the gradual glowing of autumn foliage enrich the scene and make it, for some gardeners, far more satisfying than the fragilities of spring. Fruit trees and vines are not negligible participants in the show, each variety turning to a different tone of gold, burnt orange, or even red.

Some regions, in the mountains, for example, have a short growing season—a decorative potager at the Château du Dauphin in the Auvergne, described as early as the sixteenth century by Montaigne, often feels the first frost in late August. But there are also climates that allow for a fall garden, a whole fresh crop of new potatoes, peas, carrots, onions, or spinach (once again possible in the south with cooler temperatures). In some parts of France as many as three crops are grown regularly on one piece of land in a year. Of course, the professionals of intensive gardening have been known to exceed this record by far: Parisian market gardeners in the late nineteenth century, practicing intensive cultivation of the most skillful sort, got eight different harvests from their one- to two-acre potagers, year after year. But each was always a balance of only two crops at a time, cauliflower underplanted with lettuce, for example. The orchestration of many different vegetables in a decorative potager requires mastery of a high order.

The unfolding of the seasons in such a plot ought ideally to resemble the cooking Marcel Proust remembered from his childhood. Changing throughout the year, it echoed those "quatrefoils that were sculpted on the portals of cathedrals in the thirteenth century," a series of pictures, all elegant harmony, "that reflect a bit the rhythm of the seasons and the episodes of life." Few gardeners will realize this ambition completely, but as the garden scenes evolve, there will be much to admire and much to enjoy.

❧ The manure-enriched soil at the Château de Miromesnil produces abundant harvests of beautiful vegetables. Many gardeners consider that potagers reach their peak of beauty in autumn, whereas strictly ornamental gardens are often best in late spring or early summer.

REPOSE

Vegetable gardeners often regard their plots of leeks and beans as a refuge from toil and care—in spite of the backbreaking tasks they accomplish there. English writer Ford Madox Ford noted the powerful attraction of the potager for spare-time activity when passing through the small town of Tarascon in the 1930's: " . . . the Tarasconnais, like the Parisian and like myself, is an inveterate kitchen gardener . . . the moment the shades of evening begin to fall he is up and away from desk or counter and wading amongst the profusion of his melon-patch, his pumpkins, his gourdes, pimenti and his tomatoes. . . . " Many devotees spend all their spare time, even vacations, slaving over their vegetables, and look forward to continuing their efforts at retirement. All so-called leisure moments may be engrossed by this passion.

WORK AND PLAY

Western culture insists on distinctions between work and rest, work and play, job and vacation, distinctions that become problematic and even meaningless in the

garden. A decorative potager, even more than the utilitarian variety, requires work; but it is a welcoming place, a haven, a repose for the eye as for the mind, a kind of small Eden. And if it is not a paradise where one sits around plucking fruit, forbidden or not, it is still a bad day when the gardener does not experience his or her own small plot as idyllic.

For although the decorative vegetable garden involves constant effort, it is often said that in such a domain one does not feel time passing. Just being there is restful. Vegetable gardeners often look with scorn on such strenuous sports as tennis. "Digging, penetrating into, breaking up the earth is a labor—a pleasure, an exaltation that sterile sports can never know," wrote Colette. Sportsmen might reply that they can enjoy their leisure when they feel like it; a garden will not wait. Yet perhaps much of the vegetable gardener's sense of repose comes from this compelling connection with the very cycle of the seasons.

Play in the garden is a more unusual concept, but closely linked to the pleasure Colette describes. An idyllic garden can create a sense of childish delight—

☙ *ABOVE:* **A basket of lilacs and spring vegetables, so tender that most can be eaten raw, makes every effort worthwhile. They give almost more pleasure than the generous bounties of autumn.**

☙ *OPPOSITE:* **Most vegetable gardens possess a bench along one side, made of local materials whenever possible. But how often does the gardener actually sit down and look at the fruits of his or her labor?**

although this dimension, like aesthetic enjoyment generally in the potager, may work against maximum efficiency in the serious business of producing crops. The element of play has inspired several landscape architects at the Conservatoire du

🌿 *ABOVE:* **The Island Potager created at Chaumont in 1994 by Bernard Chapuis and Georges Vafias for the Agence Européenne de Paysage shows how vegetables can be decorative in delightful new ways.**
🌿 *OPPOSITE:* **An amusing scarecrow protected the Farmyard Garden at Chaumont in 1993. Few garden inhabitants allow such scope for the playful imagination as this character.**

Paysage at the Château de Chaumont. In 1992, an experimental potager was made by the children of a local grade school. In one part, visitors were invited to sow parallel strips of land with whatever they wanted, producing unexpected patterns.

The Island Vegetable Garden project created in 1994 at Chaumont by architect Georges Vafias and landscaper Bernard Chapuis for the Agence Euro-péene de Paysage featured six square beds of beautiful vegetables set in shallow tin tubs, floating in a pond. Three more squares contained beautifully arrayed, sunken, clear glass bottles, which helped heat up the water and hence the soil of the tubs. These were filled with exotic vegetables—peanuts, sugarcane, citronella, yams, sweet potatoes, and ginger among them—the climbers supported on bamboo tents. Surrounding the pond was a miniature desert landscape. The whole space was a kind of Robinson Crusoe adventure. But all the playful details, like the solar-heated bottles, were both ornamental and practical at the same time. Bicycle pumps installed near the entrance allowed visitors to blow bubbles to oxygenate the water, which was otherwise stagnant. Other pumps let guests squirt water on the foliage of the plants—which, in that particularly hot summer, much needed this small attention. Many visitors, of course, squirted the water on each other instead. In 1994 landscapers' projects at Chaumont were variously named "The Princess's Elephant," "The Garden of Giant Leaves," or "The Hostile, Dare-Devil Garden," among others with more conventional themes. The spirit of play, of childlike invention and discovery, is alive and well at Chaumont.

The domestic cat, a frequent garden companion, provides an intriguing model for both play and repose. Pierre Gascar explains the appeal of feline friends in his *jardin de curé:* "By their movements and poses, these cats bring to this little garden, which much needs it, the dimension of a savanna or a jungle . . . they introduce into this walled space devoted to leeks and tulips the thrill and perverse hopes of ambush, the beatitude enjoyed in the depths of a secret refuge, they incorporate thus into my modest garden the fantastic domain that any feline dream represents."

Cats have a special rapport with plants, which they love to inspect, sniff, and sometimes taste. A number of plants are said to intoxicate them, though not all animals are equally susceptible. Those of the catnip family (*nepetas*) are the best known of course, but old Japanese texts allude to the effects of the silver vine, called matatabi or *Actinidia polygama.* The stimulating properties of certain valerians and germanders have also been noted. Scientists claim that the element in valerian oil that excites cats can be scented by them when its concentration in air is as little as one part in a billion. Certainly cats are reputed to have finely tuned noses and connoisseurs' tastes. Nineteenth-century Romantic writer Théophile Gautier much admired his Seraphita when, "with little spasms of pleasure, she bit handkerchiefs impregnated with scent."

Cats' curiosity about everything that happens in the garden, its most minute, day-to-day changes, make them more than mere spectators. They are great investigators of space and dimension, and can reveal to the gardener secret corners and new perspectives. Some observers comment on the cat's acute perceptions of sound and static electricity— a cat will certainly give warning of arriving visitors before the gardener hears them come. Some writers feel that a cat can predict the weather, distant storms, or oncoming cold. Colette's mother had a theory about cats in winter curling up, nose to tail, against a slight draft, but sitting sphinx-like, with their paws turned inward, when they sensed the arrival of a strong cold front. However that may be, the cat that keeps company with the owner of a decorative vegetable garden offers one great asset: It becomes a most beautiful piece of garden sculpture, its poses and attitudes ever renewed, appearing in surprising places, ever elegant. Two cats playing together can be so beautiful that the gardener will have to stop work, sit on a bench, and watch.

And what sort of bench will this be? Most decorative vegetable gardens contain seats that afford a view on the passing show. In placing benches, the gardener must ask: Where are the views best? Where are strollers most likely to want a break in the itinerary? Seats and benches must be comfortable—old cottage gardens regularly had moss seats. Some gardeners like to plant thyme or chamomile, others prefer surfaces that can be kept dry. Stone and wood are common materials.

Styles vary, from the simple benches of the Château de Villandry set under intricate canopies of sixteenth-century latticework, to the slab of stone set at one end of the long, walled, two-part potager at La Massonnière near Le Mans, or the pairs of white-painted wooden benches at each end of chef Marc Meneau's potager in Vézelay. Painted iron furniture is popular (though it needs upkeep): A green table and some chairs sit at the heart of Jean Bardet's herb garden, providing a comfortable vantage point on the entire garden.

Seating should take account of back support. If plants are allowed to tumble over from a wall behind, the gardener may not realize—admiring how they look—that they prevent the visitor from leaning back comfortably. Even if the gardener never takes time to sit down (and this is a shame but perhaps not uncommon), he or she should try out the benches and keep them in order.

Benches must be sheltered—from prevailing winds and perhaps also, in hot climates, from the sun. Benches under a trelliswork supporting vines and roses are most traditional in French gardens. A wonderful example, at the Château de Saint-Jean-de-Beauregard near Paris, supports immense ramblers like 'Kiftsgate' and 'Tobie Tristam'.

NIGHT

Work, play, and repose remain thus all intermingled, more perhaps in the decorative potager than in any other garden. (Even the cats work, of course, but at night when most gardeners are asleep.) A good deal of garden activity continues at night, when plants cool off in midsummer and twilight watering penetrates the soil before evaporating as it would in the heat of the sun. Yet in the night garden there is also repose: Poet Francis Ponge imagines plants after dark exuding carbon dioxide "like a sigh of satisfaction lasting hours on end."

Gardeners who enjoy a moonlight stroll in the cool of the evening should plant scented, white flowers such as the tall decorative tobacco plants (*Nicotiana*) or moon vines (*Ipomoea alba*). In the south, the perennial *Datura arborea* opens huge white trumpets that lift themselves up to be smelled (but never tasted, this plant is highly poisonous). Silver foliage plants can also be effective. Bruno Goris, the Riviera gardener whose vegetables thrive behind hedges of Neapolitan santolina,

❧ The variety of benches to be found in French potagers is infinite, from the elaborate fretwork gracing the long herb borders of a refined Provençal garden to a simple wooden slab set on two logs at the Château de Miromesnil, to the comfortable and unassuming park bench in Marc Meneau's gastronomic potager. All of these gardens receive many visitors, who are grateful for the vantage points and resting places.

finds the latter's glow a great help when he dashes out to pick last-minute salad greens after dark.

Ornamental potagers, like other gardens, may be lighted by fixtures more reliable than silver foliage in the moonlight, at least along paths and walls. Some gardeners like ground-level fixtures that are invisible by day. Landscaper Jean Mus partially encloses lamps between two curved terracotta tiles set at the foot of a tree so that the light shines on both the path and the gnarled trunk. Others prefer something more showy and seasonal, like the torches on bamboo stakes commonly sold in summer, easily stuck in the ground and moved around the garden at will for special celebrations. Lighting depends on the use to which the garden will be put and how much time will be spent there in the evenings—whether to dine outdoors, or for a leisurely walk, or simply for a quick raid on the herb patch.

Japanese gardens sometimes include platforms for moon watching. Many French gardeners closely follow the cycles of the moon not only for its beauty but for its effects in planning various gardening activities. The ancient sources are at variance on the subject of lunar influence, however: Renaissance writer Pierre de Crescens described Adam's explaining to Cain the importance of the moon's phases in sowing and growing, digging and pruning, but Olivier de Serres remained doubtful, as did La Quintinye later on. Nonetheless, today, two of France's most popular vegetable gardening magazines, *Rustica* and *Les Quatre saisons,* regularly give advice on and provide calendars for gardening by the moon.

At night the garden has a life of its own. The frog chorus begins suddenly, reliably, according to changing temperature, at twilight. A host of creatures make the garden their own by moonlight: black and yellow sala-

☙ *Nicotiana* at Saint-Jean-de-Beauregard bursts irrepressibly out of the greenhouse windows, sending its powerful perfume far and wide.

⅋ *RIGHT & OVERLEAF:* **At twilight, garden scents are especially alluring, none more than that of the ornamental tobacco plant (*Nicotiana*). Often the white variety is planted because white flowers stand out against the fading light, at a time when reds become almost invisible. This is especially true for the dull-textured plumes of *Amaranthus*, so striking during the day (here shown at Saint-Jean-de-Beauregard, both red- and green-leafed varieties).**

manders, which count among the world's oldest vertebrates, circling bats, clumsy toads, all good predators of garden pests. A nocturnal visitor to the garden may be lucky enough to meet some of its night-dwelling inhabitants . . . and may in any case with pleasure remember the lines of William Blake:

> *The moon like a flower,*
> *In heaven's high bower,*
> *With silent delight,*
> *Sets and smiles on the night.*

WINTER

The great time of rest for the garden itself is winter, though it is the rest of hibernation, in which vital processes slow down but never cease. And yet potagers can be very beautiful in winter, in spite of bouts of digging and manuring and even planting if the climate allows. Often the light in winter can be pure magic. Someone as ill tuned to gardening as Oscar Wilde could write: "There are winter days so full of sudden sunlight that they will cheat the wise crocus into squandering its gold before its time." In southern France especially, where the mistral, the fierce north wind, gusts for days on end, it brings with it a golden clarity that seems almost palpable.

In all parts of France, leeks and cabbages can stay in the ground over winter, and these count among the most decorative vegetables. The 'Bleu de Solaise' variety of leek is highly resistant to cold and to bugs, and has a special, attractive, metallic blue tinge that takes on hints of red as well. Kale (including the ornamental red, white, and green kind), brussels sprouts (red and green), and broccoli

(especially the exquisite Romanesco variety) all look good in the winter garden, and any left uneaten may be allowed to flower in early spring. Cold intensifies their colors, but too sudden a thaw can do damage.

In many parts of France, hardy varieties of lettuce survive outdoors in winter. The famous salad blend mesclun is a Provençal winter mix, and its ingredients (*roquette* or arugula, *mâche* or corn salad, radicchio or red-leafed chicory, escarole or curly endives) all overwinter in the south, as does spinach. This mix makes a pretty salad, and can also be decorative growing in the winter garden. It is said that smaller rosettes of mâche resist the cold better than the large ones, which should be eaten first. The improved version of wild chicory, known as "sugar loaf" or *pain de sucre,* is one of the hardiest salad greens, since the heart can be eaten even if the outside deteriorates. When left to flower, it produces blossoms of an almost electric blue. And of course, many gardeners force endives in pots indoors, the result being delicious both raw and as a cooked vegetable.

Gardeners can easily slip a few tulip bulbs, wallflowers, or pansies in among rows of salad greens that are expected to remain through early spring. They can be moved elsewhere without much trouble when the next crop is sown.

Taken from the ground in mild regions or from storage in the north, a wide range of root vegetables keep the potager present on the winter table: carrots ('Chantenay' or 'Colmar' varieties), turnips ('Blanc dur d'hiver'), beets, and black radishes. Parsnips in France are a collector's item; the variety 'Demi-long de Guernesey' seems to be the only one currently available. Root celery is also prized by some gardeners ('Boule de marbre', or marble ball, is the evocative name of one good variety). Most of these make good salads as well as hot vegetables—even beets, often eaten grated raw in France.

⁘ *ABOVE:* **Parsnips, common in the United States and once well known in France, are coming back into favor. In parts of France, they can be left in the ground through the winter, to be harvested as needed.**
⁘ *OPPOSITE:* **At the Château of Saint-Jean-de-Beauregard, both edible and decorative cabbages withstand the effects of a very beautiful hoarfrost.**

Stored in a dry place, potatoes and beans lend themselves to many winter preparations. British horticulturalist William Robinson, visiting the Paris markets in 1868, noted the importance of the latter, "grown and used to a degree of which we can have but a poor conception" and "used every day in winter, in the smallest as well as in the grandest restaurants." Some of the varieties he noted, like the green flageolet of Laon, are still available, but others, like the black Algerian bean, are sadly lacking today.

Vegetables that overwinter can be sown or planted in raised ridges, and mulched about 4 inches thick with straw or dead leaves or bracken. This can be done with attention to line and pattern, just as in summer plantings, even though winter weather can make it hard to keep things neat. This is where evergreen edgers like dwarf box, rosemary, or strawberries, or paths of stone or brick, help a good deal, keeping a strong outline even when the vegetation is variable.

Some vegetables need to be wrapped, like shrubs or trees. Cardoons intended for the table usually have their stalks bundled up in newspapers, a not very aesthetic solution. This is to blanch them for eating rather than to protect them from the cold. Left unblanched and therefore uneaten, they make tall, luxuriant, gray-green fountains of foliage throughout the winter. Artichokes often have their central leaves tied together before being surrounded with straw as insulation against frost, and this can be done quite elegantly. Indeed, wrapping plants for winter can become quite an art and one that has attracted the attention of sculptors as well as gardeners. Landscaper Dominique Lafourcade, in Provence, uses the semi-rigid bamboo mats called *canisse* (usually meant to provide summer shade) around large terracotta pots containing olive trees. Thus the pots seem to support a formal cylinder of bamboo, and the trees are safe from sudden drops in temperature.

Cold frames are a traditional appurtenance to the French potager, along with the greenhouse, usually set together in one corner or at the end farthest from the house. Every château garden has a row of frames. The most beautiful are unfortunately those that use the most perishable materials: glass and wood. But these are also perhaps the easiest and cheapest to build for the home garden. Harder to get and keep are the marvelous, antique glass bells, or *cloches,* that cover winter lettuces and in late spring protect young tomato plants or eggplant. In the south, gardeners daring to set tomatoes out in March may shelter them with terracotta roof tiles set upright into the earth, each one curving around the young plant like a miniature wall. This too can make a pretty pattern.

In France as elsewhere, gardeners debate how to treat the winter potager. Should it be left bare after digging, allowing frost to break up the big clumps? Or should it be

❧ At Saint-Jean-de-Beauregard, all the wonderful cucurbits have long since been brought indoors, including Siamese squash, devil's claw, and Turk's turban, many of which will last indoors through the cold season.

REPOSE

kept covered with manure or with a green manure—either one that frost will kill in preparation for digging in, such as mustard, phacelia, certain clovers, or one that will overwinter, like crimson clover, rye, or a mixture of rye and winter vetch? These masses of vegetation can be ornamental, but some people also find bare, freshly plowed earth very beautiful—it appears in so many colors and textures.

Frost itself can add beauty, if it is not too destructive. Pierre Gascar admires frost flowers on an old stone bench. Of course, some parts of France do get snowed in, though it is rare for snow to remain on the ground for months, except in the mountains. Some sort of evergreen hedging showing up through snow makes a wonderful garden picture. And, as one expert points out, snow nicely covers up the debris that has not yet found its way to the compost. Snow is considered very beneficial for the soil, called "poor man's manure" in some parts. In Paris snow comes with the southeast wind, and local lore holds that "February snow is worth half-manure, but March snow is worth a park" (*Neige de février vaut demi-fumier, neige de mars vaut un parc*).

Snow falls most often in February in France, during those days which, in the words of one venerable gardener, "don't give much small change." But there can be flowers in the garden then too, all over the country: Witchhazels (*Hamamelis*) and early-flowering dogwoods (*Cornus mas*) give much pleasure. The latter is used to great effect in the medieval garden of the Prieuré de Salagon. The stalwart *Viburnum bodnantense* 'Dawn', which makes a nondescript sort of bush most of the year, brims over with pink bloom for weeks on end in February and March. All southern gardens have at least one bush of *Viburnum laurustinus,* the flowers of which are pink in bud and white when they open, against dark green foliage. They mix beautifully with the

☙ There are garden lovers who actually prefer winter, as a time of soft colors and light, when well-designed gardens show off their "good bones." Tree shapes can be haunting in winter, especially when as carefully trained as these cordons at Saint-Jean-de-Beauregard.

dark blue flowers of Corsican rosemary (the cascading variety) and the strong, elegant design of Corsican hellebores with their lime-green, bell-like blossoms. Laurustinus and rosemary make good hedge and wall plants, and this composition is easy to accomplish on the edge of the potager where the climate allows.

Winter climbers light up a corner of any garden—the liquid gold of winter jasmine, or the billowing white mounds of the lesser-known *Clematis balearica.* Since the latter may get a bit bare and mildewed in summer, it should be planted with something that will shield it later on. Bruno Goris grows it up a white-blooming Judas tree near the entrance to his Riviera potager, so that the tree will flower when the vine has stopped. Clumps of white-flowered Japanese anemones hide the feet of both tree and clematis.

Winter-blooming iris can make a partial edger somewhere too: The Algerian, or *stylosa,* variety quickly makes dense lines, and gives pleasure with pale or dark blue flowers from November to March.

Fruit trees can also add much to the winter decor. British expert Mirabel Osler in her book on garden walls wrote about espaliered trees: "Even in winter, when the bare branches are spread out neat as fishbones, you have no need to be wishing it was some other month." In the south, persimmons hang like bright orange Christmas decorations on black branches in January. They must be dead ripe to eat without making the mouth pucker with astringency, and it is hard to get them before the birds do. Professional growers pick them early and let them ripen indoors, but it is hard for an ornamental gardener to remove them from the tree where they are so beautiful.

Hedges can be planned to feed birds in winter: Any of the berry-bearing varieties, such as pyracantha, will offer a feast and remain decorative until stripped. Others have been developed on purpose to be unappealing to birds, so that the ornamental effect lasts longer.

In the paradise garden imagined nine centuries before Christ by the Greek poet Homer, there was no winter, for mild westerly breezes simply brought on crop after crop for eternity. Some gardeners might yearn for this magic land, but many would miss the beauty of winter for its own sake. Oriental poet Yüan Mee was one of these: "O, my garden gleaming cold and white, thou has outshone the far faint moon on high." If for every thing there is a season, then the season of repose is not the least appealing, even for northern gardeners, poring over seed catalogues and wondering if they will ever see spring again. But while the poets disagree, the gardener has no choice: Winter will come and should be treated with respect, courted also for the beauty and benefits it can provide.

Here, as in so much else, the last word should be reserved for that great southern French gardener Olivier de Serres, pondering how much work his garden projects required: "One should stop there where one finds the greatest profit and pleasure."

IDEAS FOR DESIGNING THE POTAGER

These lists are meant only to offer suggestions for potager design, but they are certainly not exhaustive of the possibilities. Plants cited here may perform differently in different climates and regions as to height and volume, even color and the need for support.

EDGERS FOR OUTLINING BEDS

LOW EDGERS

ANNUALS: dwarf basils, including red varieties 'Dark Opal' and 'Purple Ruffles'; beets; dwarf marigolds; dwarf nasturtiums (perhaps mixed with beets); curly parsley; many lettuce varieties, particularly the "cut-and-come-again" ones.

PERENNIALS: sweet woodruff (*Asperula odorata*), cottage pinks (*Dianthus plumarius*), rabbit ears (*Stachys lanata*), germander (*Teucrium germander*); low-growing catnip, chives, bush thyme, violets.

MEDIUM EDGERS

ANNUALS: taller varieties of basil, bush beans, red cabbage, dwarf dahlias, pot marigolds, summer savory.

PERENNIALS: bee balm (*Melissa*), dwarf box, catnip (*Nepeta faassini*), hyssop, dwarf irises, dwarf lavenders, garden sage in several colors (*Salvia officinalis*), winter savory (*Satureja montana*), strawberries.

TALL EDGERS

ANNUALS: broccoli, cauliflower; cosmos, lavatera, tall-growing marigolds, and many other flowers; some fragrant pelargoniums; sweet and hot peppers; Swiss chard (white, red, or yellow ribbed).

PERENNIALS: low-growing cistus, dahlias, gladiolus, dwarf hebes, lavenders, rosemaries, rue, santolinas, *Sedum spectabile*.

POTAGER PLANTS BY SIZE, SHAPE, AND HABIT

VERTICAL ACCENTS

WITHOUT SUPPORT: amaranths, angelica, artichokes, Jerusalem artichokes, asparagus, bay laurel (pruned), many cabbage family plants (Brassicas), cannas, cardoons, clary sage (*Salvia sclarea*), sweet corn, delphiniums, fennel (green and bronze), hollyhocks, horseradish, lemon verbena, orach (red or green), *Phlomis samia*, standard roses, rosemary, rhubarb, sunflowers, Mexican sunflower (*Tithonia*), ornamental tobacco, verbascums, *Verbena bonariensis*; small fruit bushes grown as standards.

NEEDING SUPPORT: asparagus beans, runner beans, snow peas; cucurbits on trellises; Malabar spinach; tomatoes; espaliered or cordon fruit trees; morning glories, climbing nasturtiums, sweet peas and other annual climbers; blackberry vine, chayote, grapevines, hops, kiwi, and small fruit bushes grown on wires; honeysuckle, climbing and rambling roses.

UNUSUAL FRUIT TREES: fig, jujube, loquat, medlar, mulberry, quince, persimmon, pomegranate.

dwarf buddleia; chaste tree (*Vitex*); dwarf ornamental almonds, apples, cherries, or peach; escallonia; Persian or Chinese lilac; mock orange (*Philadelphus*); shrub and standard roses; smaller viburnums.

ARCHITECTURAL PLANTS HAVING STRONG DESIGN IN GROWTH HABIT OR FOLIAGE

Artichokes, broccoli, bush beans, cannas, cardoons, cauliflower, ground cherry or cape gooseberry, corn, cucumber when staked, fennel, hellebores (various), kale, leeks, pak choy, sweet and hot peppers, okra, rhubarb, rue, *Sedum spectabile*, spurges (*Euphorbias*, various), sunflowers, tomatoes when staked.

BUSHY OR CLUMP-FORMING EVERGREEN PLANTS

Dwarf box, cistus, chrysanthemums, curry plant (*Helichrysum*), germander, dwarf hebes, hyssop, irises, lavenders, dwarf pittosporum, rosemaries (bush and creeping), rue, winter savory, *Sedum spectabile*, sorrel, bush thymes.

FEATHERY FOLIAGE

Asparagus, carrots, cumin, dill, fennel.

CURLY FOLIAGE

Curly endive, kale, curly parsley.

SELF-SOWERS

Acanthus, asters, annual campanulas, chervil, columbines, coreopsis, corn cockle (*Agrostemma githago*), cosmos, digitalis, echinops, *Erigeron mucronatus*, evening primrose, fennel, feverfew, gaillardia, gaura, geum, hellebores, hollyhocks, honesty, larkspur, lavatera, lettuces, purple loosestrife, love-in-a-mist (*Nigella damascena*), lupin, lychnis, mallows, marigolds, Mexican poppy (*Eschscholtzia*), dwarf morning glory (*Convolvulus tricolor*), muscari, mustard, narcissus, nicotiana, orach, oregano, phacelia, phlomis, poppies, spurges (*Euphorbia characias*, snow-in-summer or *Euphorbia marginata*, *E.myrsinites*, *E.lathyris*, *E.polychroma*), sweet peas, toad flax, tulips and many other spring bulbs, false valerian (*Centranthus*), verbascums, veronicas, violets, Virginian stock (*Malcomia maritima*), wallflowers.

FAST FILLERS

Sweet alyssum, chervil, cosmos, garden cress, mustard, phacelia, salad transplants, bedding plants.

THE PALETTE OF VEGETABLE AND HERB COLORS

RED, PURPLE, OR BLUE-VIOLET

FOLIAGE: amaranth (love-lies-bleeding or prince's-feather); purple basils; red Brussels sprouts, cabbages, cauliflower, kohlrabi; rhubarb chard; red-tinged lettuces like batavia, oak-leaf, or newer varieties such as American red 'Salad Bowl', Italian 'Lollo rosso', red chicory or radicchio; bronze mustard; red orach; *Perilla frutescens*; purple-leafed garden sage.

FRUIT: purple-podded beans, purple-sprouting broccoli, red brussels sprouts, eggplant, peppers, tomatoes; red gooseberries, raspberries, strawberries.

FLOWER: artichoke and cardoon flowers, scarlet runner bean, borage, lavender, purple-flowered peas, *Phacelia tanacetifolia*.

YELLOW

FOLIAGE: yellow-leafed varieties of bee balm, celery, oregano, and garden sage.

FRUIT: some varieties of butter beans, peppers, amber raspberries, many varieties of squash and pumpkin, tomatoes.

FLOWERS: Jerusalem artichokes, most of the cabbage family, squash and pumpkin, sunflowers.

BLUE OR BLUE-GREEN

FOLIAGE: broad beans, many cabbages, leeks, rue, seakale.

FLOWERS: chicory, *Phacelia campanularia.*

SILVER AND WHITE

FOLIAGE: artemisias, artichokes, cardoons, curry plant, lavender, santolina.

FRUIT: cauliflower, white eggplant, white kohlrabi, some squashes.

FLOWERS: many bean and pea varieties, leeks and onions, white lavender.

FLOWERS FOR THE POTAGER

BLUE AND PURPLE FLOWERS

Anenomes, bachelor's buttons (*Centaurea*), bluebells, borage, cobea, columbines, cynoglossum, delphinium, echinops, eryngium, perennial flax, gillia, hyssop, larkspur, lavender, love-in-a-mist, morning glory (*Ipomoea*), nepetas, nierembergia, Oswego tea (*Monarda*), some penstemons, perennial flax, perovskia, petunia, phacelia, platycodon, rosemary, garden sage, *Salvia hormium,* scabious, stokesia, sweet alyssum, verbenas, veronicas, violets.

PINK FLOWERS

Anemones, asters, cleomes, dianthus, digitalis, godetia, gyposphila, larkspur, lavatera, saponaria (invasive), wild false valerian (*Centranthus*), verbenas.

RED FLOWERS

Cannas, geum, helianthus, heuchera, nasturtiums, penstemons, Mexican sunflower (*Tithonia*), false valerian (*Centranthus ruber*).

YELLOW AND ORANGE FLOWERS

Coreopsis, California poppy (*Eschscholztia*), evening primrose (*Oenoethera*), gazanias, geum, goldenrod (invasive), helianthus, marigolds, nasturtiums, painted tongue (*Salpiglossis*), pot marigolds, rudbeckia, wallflowers.

GREEN FLOWERS

Mollucella, nicotiana, zinnia 'Green Envy'.

WHITE FLOWERS

Anemones, actinidias (including kiwi), white varieties of *Centranthus* and love-in-a-mist, gypsophila, scabious, sweet alyssum.

MANY COLORS

Asters, chrysanthemums, columbines, dahlias, hollyhocks, irises, lupins, nicotiana, roses, zinnias.

DESIGNING
THE POTAGER

COMPANION PLANTS—
AND PAIRINGS TO AVOID

AMARANTH: with corn, onions, potatoes.

ASPARAGUS: with cucumbers, leeks, parsley, peas; but not with beets, garlic, or onions.

BEANS: with beets, cabbage, cucumber, lettuce, squash, tomatoes; but not with garlic, leeks, onions, or shallot.

BEETS: with beans, cabbage, lettuce; but not with tomatoes.

CABBAGE: with beans, beets, celery, cucumber, peas, potatoes, squash, tomatoes; but not with fennel, garlic, leeks, radishes, or strawberries.

CARROTS AND PARSNIPS: with garlic, onions, leeks, peas, radishes, shallots.

CELERY: with cabbage, cucumber, lettuce, peas, potatoes, tomatoes.

CORN: with beans, peas, squash, tomatoes; but not with beets, celery, or potatoes.

GARLIC: with potatoes, roses, strawberries; but not with carrots, cabbage, or peas.

ONIONS: with carrots, parsnips, strawberries, tomatoes; but not with beans or peas.

PEAS: with cabbage, celery, potatoes; but not with onions or tomatoes.

POTATOES: with cabbage, peas; but not with garlic, leeks, or onions.

SQUASH AND PUMPKINS: with beans, cabbage, corn, lettuce, potatoes.

STRAWBERRIES: with garlic, leeks, mâche, onions, shallots, spinach; but not with cabbages.

TOMATOES: with beans, cabbage, celery, garlic, leeks, onions, parsley, shallots.

SEED SOURCES

Following are some seed sources for French vegetable varieties and collector's items mentioned in these pages.

UNITED STATES

FOR MORE ESOTERIC FRENCH VEGETABLES

COOK'S GARDEN, Box 535, Londonderry, VT 05148. TEL: 802-824-3400. FAX: 802-824-3027.

LE JARDIN DU GOURMET, P.O. Box 7WP, St. Johnsbury, VT 05863.
TEL: 802-748-1446. FAX: 802-748-9592.

JOHNNY'S SELECTED SEEDS, Foss Hill Road, Albion, ME 04910. TEL: 207-437-4301.
FAX: 207-437-2615.

REDWOOD CITY SEED COMPANY, P.O. Box 361, Redwood City, CA 94064. TEL: 415-325-7333.

SHEPHERD'S GARDEN SEEDS, 30 Irene Street, Torrington, CT 06790. TEL: 203-482-3638.
FAX: 203-482-0532.

FOR BETTER-KNOWN FRENCH VEGETABLES

BURPEE, 300 Park Avenue, Warminster, PN 18974. TEL: 800-888-1447.
FAX: 800-487-5530.

HARRIS SEEDS, 60 Saginaw Drive, P.O. Box 22960, Rochester, NY 14692-2960.
TEL: 800-514-4441. FAX: 716-442-9386.

PINETREE GARDEN SEEDS, Box 300, New Gloucester, ME 04260. TEL: 207-926-3400.
FAX: 207-926-3886.

FOR FLOWERS, HERBS, AND FRUIT TREES

J.L. HUDSON, **Seedsman**, P.O. Box 1058, Redwood City, CA 94064.

NORTHWOODS RETAIL NURSERY, 27635 S. Oglesby Road, Canby, OR 97013.
TEL: 503-266-5432. FAX: 503-266-5431.

PARK SEED COMPANY, Cokesbury Road, Greenwood, SC 29647. TEL: 803-223-7333/
800-845-3361. FAX: 800-275-9941.

THOMPSON & MORGAN, P.O. Box 1308, Jackson, NJ 08527. TEL: 908-363-2225.

WELL-SWEEP HERB FARM, 317 Mt. Bethel Road, Port Murray, NJ 07865. TEL: 908-852-5390.

FRANCE

BAUMAUX GRAINES, 11, rue des 4 Eglises, B.P. 590, 54009 Nancy. TEL: 83 32 01 67. FAX 83 35 57 70.

BIAU GERME, 47360 Montpezat d'Agenais. TEL: 53 95 09 07.

CLUB MÉMOIRE VERTE. B.P. 20, 33670 La Sauve-Majeure.

COMPTOIR DES JARDINIERS DE FRANCE. B.P. 559, 59308 Valenciennes.
TEL: 27 46 37 50.

FERME DE SAINTE MARTHE SARL, B.P. 10, 41700 Cour-Cheverny. TEL: 54 44 20 03.

LA SCOUTINERIE, Attn. Mr. A. Fert, 86, La Maladrerie, 26110 Nyons. TEL: 75 26 33 52.
(For crocosemis, or sisal netting, to keep ground moist after sowing.)

THOMPSON AND MORGAN IN FRANCE: La Meiletière, 61150 St. Ouen-sur-Maire.
TEL: 33 35 85 00.

GARDENS CITED OPEN TO THE PUBLIC

AUBERGE DES CIMES (RESTAURANT), 43290 Saint-Bonnet-le-Froid. Owner and chef: René Marcon. TEL: 71 59 93 72. FAX: 71 59 93 40. (Country inn, small mountain village west of Rhône Valley. Chef specializing in rare vegetables. Herb garden being created.)

CHÂTEAU DE DAUPHIN, 63230 Pontgibaud. Owners: M. and Mme. Gabriel de Germiny. TEL: 73 88 73 39. (Auvergne, west of Clermont-Ferrand.)

CHÂTEAU DE GALLEVILLE, 76560 Doudeville. Ambassador and Mrs. Robert Gillet. TEL: 35 96 54 65. Gardens open afternoons from July 22 to August 31 and for groups, on request, from May to October.

CHÂTEAU DE MIROMESNIL, 76550 Tourville-sur-Arques. Owner: M. de Vogüé. TEL/FAX: 35 85 02 80. Open summers. (Normandy, 8 km south of Dieppe.)

CHÂTEAU D'OPME, 63540 Romagnat. Owners: M. and Mme. Philippe Durin. Tel: 73 87 54 85. (Auvergne, south of Clermont-Ferrand.)

CHÂTEAU DES PÊCHEURS, La Bussière. Owner: Mme. de Chasseval. TEL: 38 35 93 35. Open in summer by appointment. (Between the Loire and Burgundy, south of Paris.)

CHÂTEAU DE ROUSSAN (HOTEL), Route de Tarascon, 13210 Saint-Rémy-de-Provence. TEL: 90 92 11 63. FAX: 90 92 37 32. (Provence, between Avignon and Arles; for its greenhouse, no potager.)

CHÂTEAU DE SAINT-JEAN-DE-BEAUREGARD, 91940 Saint-Jean-de-Beauregard. Owners: M. and Mme. de Curel. TEL: 60 12 00 01. (23 km southwest of Paris. Plant fairs here in May and October.)

CHÂTEAU DE VILLANDRY, 37510 Villandry. Owner: Mr. Carvallo. TEL: 47 50 02 09. (15 km west of Tours. The most famous of French ornamental potagers.)

CONSERVATOIRE INTERNATIONAL DES PARCS ET JARDINS ET DU PAYSAGE, Ferme du Château de Chaumont, 41150 Chaumont-sur-Loire. TEL: 54 20 99 22. FAX: 54 20 99 24. (Loire Valley. Thirty new experimental gardens each year, including at least one potager.)

BRUNO GORIS (garden consultant), Chemin du Paradis, 06620 Le Bar-sur-Loup. TEL: 93 42 55 17. Garden open summers on Sunday. (Côte d'Azur, north of Nice.)

JARDIN BOTANIQUE DE LA MHOTTE, B.P. 2, 03210 St. Menoux. TEL: 70 43 96 92. FAX: 70 43 96 83.

JARDIN DES PLANTES, Montpellier, administered by the Faculty of Medecine Montpellier I. TEL: 67 63 43 22. Open every day but Sunday, schedules vary by season. (Southwest France; one of the oldest botanical gardens in the country.)

JEAN BARDET (RESTAURANT-HÔTEL), 57 rue Groison, 37000 Tours. Owners: Jean and Sophie Bardet, and Chef: Jean Bardet. TEL: 47 41 41 11. FAX: 47 51 68 72. (Loire valley. Bardet is both collector of rare vegetables and gastronome.)

LA MASSONNIÈRE, 72540 Saint-Christophe-en-Champagne-par-Loue. Owner: M. Joël Moulin. TEL: 43 88 61 26. (Near Le Mans; open most weekends.)

L'ESPÉRANCE (RESTAURANT), 89450 Saint Pierre-sous-Vézelay. Owner and chef: Marc Meneau. TEL: 86 33 20 45. FAX: 86 33 26 15. (In Burgundy, one of France's great restaurants.)

PRIEURÉ DE SALAGON, 04300 Mane. Owned by the Association Alpes de Lumière. TEL: 92 75 19 93. (Haute-Provence, west of Grasse, near Manosque. Medieval abbey with several gardens.)

DOMINIQUE SOLTNER, Le Clos Lorelle, 49130 Saint-Gemmes-sur-Loire. TEL: 41 66 38 26. FAX: 41 79 86 70. (For publications and information on rustic hedges.)

VERSAILLES, Potager du Roi, 4, rue Hardy, 78000 Versailles. TEL: 39 50 60 87; 39 02 71 03; or 39 51 61 29. (Greater Paris. Call ahead, very unpredictable schedules.)

VILLA SAINT-JEAN (CHAMBRES D'HÔTES, meals for groups with reservation), 91 Chemin Saint-Jean, 06130 Grasse. Owners: M. and Mme. Rolando. Chef: Eric Berthier. TEL/FAX: 93 77 92 69. (Côte d'Azur. Beautiful eighteenth-century house; workshops, including "Flowers and Savors.")

VILLEJUIF (TOWN OF). Municipally owned garden plots rented out to inhabitants, tool sheds designed by Renzo Piano (creator of Beaubourg Pompidou Center in Paris). Visible from the freeway.

Books Consulted

Almanach Rustica 94. Paris: Rustica, 1994.

Beucher, Patricia, and Jean-Paul Collaert. *Le Beau jardin du Paresseux.* Paris: France Inter, 1986.

Bronzert, Kathleen, and Bruce Sherwin, eds. *The Glory of the Garden.* New York: Avon, 1993.

Colette. *La Naissance du jour.* Paris: Garnier-Flammarion, 1969.

Prisons et paradis. Paris: Fayard, 1986.

Sido. Paris: Hachette, 1901.

Couplan, François. *Retrouvez les légumes oubliés.* Paris: La Maison rustique, 1986.

Defay, Bruno. *Trésors de courges et de potirons.* Paris: Editions Terre Vivante, n.d.

Ford, Ford Madox. *Provence.* London: The Ecco Press, 1962.

Fortescue, Winifred. *Perfume from Provence.* Edinburgh: William Blackwood and Sons, 1950.

Franck, Gertrud. *Cultures associées du jardin.* Paris: La Maison rustique, 1983.

Mon jardin sauvage, fleurie et productif. Paris: Terre Vivante, 1986.

Gascar, Pierre. *Un Jardin de curé.* Paris: Stock, 1979.

Givry, Jacques de, and Yves Perillon. *Versailles: Le Potager du roi.* Les Loges-en-Josas: JDG Publications, 1993.

Gouvion, Colette, and Marielle Huclie. *Le Roman du potager.* Rodez: Editions du Rouergue, 1994.

James, Henry. *A Little Tour in France.* Oxford: Oxford University Press, 1984.

Le Dantec, Denise and Jean-Pierre. *Le Roman des jardins de France: leur histoire.* Paris: Plon, 1985.

Le Jardin astucieux des quatre saisons. Paris: Terre Vivante, 1992.

Lequenne, Fernand. *Olivier de Serres: agronome et soldat de Dieu.* Paris: Berger-Levrault, 1983.

Lieutaghi, Pierre. *Jardin des savoirs, jardin d'histoire.* Mane: Les Alpes de Lumière 110-11, n.d.

Mitchell, Henry. *The Essential Earthman.* Boston: Houghton Mifflin, 1981.

Osler, Mirabel. *The Garden Wall.* New York: Simon & Schuster, 1993.

Pailleux A., and D. Bois, *Le Potager d'un curieux.* Paris: Librairie Agricole de la Maison rustique, 1892; reprinted by Editions Jeanne Laffitte, Marseilles, 1994.

Pelt, Jean-Maris. *Des Légumes,* Paris: Fayard, 1993.

Phillips, Cecilia. *Letters from Provence.* London: Garnstone Press, 1975.

Ponge, Francis. *Le Parti pris des choses.* Paris: Gallimard, 1942.

Proust, Marcel. *Du Côté de chez Swann.* Paris: Gallimard, 1954.

Quintinye, Jean de la. *The Complete Gardener,* trans. George Londs and Henry Wife, preface by J. Evelyn, 3rd edition, London, 1701.

Renaud, Victor. *Les Légumes rares et oubliés.* Paris: Rustica, 1991.

Robinson, W. *The Parks, Promenades and Gardens of Paris: Described as Considered in Relation to the Wants of Our Own Cities.* London: John Murray, 1869.

Rousseau, Jean-Jacques. *Julie, ou la nouvelle Héloïse.* Paris, Gallimard, 1968.

Salgon, Jean-Jacques. *07 et autres récits.* Paris: Verdier, 1993.

Scott-James, Anne. *The Language of the Garden.* London: Penguin, 1984.

The Pleasure Garden. London: Penguin, 1979.

Sitwell, Edith, ed. *A Book of Flowers.* London: Macmillan, 1952.

Toklas, Alice B. *The Alice B. Toklas Cook Book,* New York: Harper & Brothers, 1954.

Versepuy, Michel M. *Paradis terrestre: journal d'un jardin.* Paris: Saggitaire, 1944.

Vilmorin-Andrieux, M. *The Vegetable Garden.* English edition published under the direction of W. Robinson. Berkeley, CA.: Ten Speed Press, n.d.

RECIPE SUGGESTIONS

The following are ideas for enjoying the produce of a French-style vegetable garden. Many of these suggestions are classics of French home cooking. Just as every family has its own version of these favorites, so you too may adapt and modify them to suit your particular tastes.

CLASSIC SOUPS

❧ AÏGO BOUIDO (PROVENÇAL HERB SOUP): In a nonreactive soup pot or saucepan, cook chopped leeks, peeled and chopped ripe tomatoes, and minced garlic cloves lightly in olive oil until the leeks are tender, about 10 minutes. Pour in hot water to cover. Add sprigs each of sage, fennel, and thyme; 1 piece of orange zest; and a bay leaf. Cover and simmer over medium-high heat for 5 minutes. Remove the herb sprigs, bay leaf, and orange zest. At this point the soup can be enriched by cooking a little pasta in it or by poaching a few eggs in the broth. Place poached eggs on slices of toast in deep soup dishes and spoon broth over. Sprinkle with grated Parmesan or Swiss cheese and serve.

❧ CHINESE-STYLE VEGETABLE SOUP: Cook a batch of rice noodles in a rich meat broth until tender. Add some chopped scallions and strips of spinach or Swiss chard, and cook briefly until wilted. Add soy sauce, chopped fresh coriander, and hot pepper flakes to taste. Just before serving, stir in a lightly beaten egg.

❧ COLD CUCUMBER-YOGURT SOUP: Cut unpeeled cucumber into small cubes; sprinkle with salt and let sit in a colander to drain for 30 minutes. Rinse and transfer to a soup tureen. Add yogurt, lemon juice, pepper, and ground cumin to taste, then thin with water to desired consistency. Garnish the soup with chopped fresh parsley and chervil just before serving.

❧ GREEN VEGETABLE AND POTATO SOUP: In a nonreactive soup pot or saucepan, sauté a generous amount of a washed leafy green vegetable—spinach, garden cress, watercress, sorrel, radish greens, or nettles—in butter until just wilted. Add an equal amount of peeled potato cubes and pour in enough water or broth to cover. Bring to a boil, then cook over medium-high heat until the potatoes are very tender, about 10 minutes. Use a food mill or blender to puree the soup. If desired, add milk or cream to enrich the soup. Garnish with a sprinkling of the chopped raw green vegetable just before serving.

❧ LEEK AND POTATO SOUP: Combine equal amounts of sliced leeks (the white part with just a bit of green for color) and cubes of peeled potato in a large saucepan or soup pot. Pour in enough cold water or bouillon to cover. Add salt to taste and cook over medium heat until the potatoes are tender, about 10 minutes. Puree in a blender or food processor, then add water, milk, or cream to reach desired consistency.

❧ POTAGE BONNE FEMME: Melt butter in a large saucepan or soup pot over medium heat. Add chopped carrots, leeks, and onions and cook until softened, about 5 minutes. Add cubes of peeled potato and pour in enough cold water to cover. Season with salt and bring to a boil. Immediately reduce the heat to low and simmer for about 30 minutes. Puree in a blender or food processor until smooth, then enrich with milk or cream, if desired.

❧ PUMPKIN OR SQUASH SOUP: Peel a small pumpkin or winter squash, remove the seeds, and cut the flesh into 1½ to 2-inch pieces. Place in a large saucepan or soup pot and add salt, a bay leaf, a finely chopped medium onion, and a thinly sliced leek (white part only). Pour in enough cold water to cover and cook over medium-low heat until the squash is tender, about 15 minutes. Remove the bay leaf. Puree in a blender or food processor, then stir in a small amount of milk to enrich the soup. Stir in some crushed garlic just before serving.

❧ SOUPE AU PISTOU: Combine chopped onion, carrot, zucchini, peeled potato and tomato, green beans, and fresh shell beans (white and pinto) in a large soup pot or saucepan. Add water to cover and simmer until all the ingredients are tender, about 30 minutes. Meanwhile, puree a bunch of basil leaves with some chopped garlic and olive oil until smooth. Remove soup from the heat and swirl in the basil paste just before serving.

COLD DISHES FEATURING VEGETABLES

❧ ARTICHOKE HEARTS: Mix artichoke hearts with chopped fresh herbs, green olives, and capers. Toss with vinaigrette.

❧ ASPARAGUS: Cook the trimmed spears until tender and dip into a soft-boiled egg or serve with a dressing of lemon juice and olive oil.

❧ BELGIAN ENDIVE, WALNUTS, BEETS, AND APPLE SALAD: Slice apples and Belgian endive and mix with walnuts and cubes of cooked beets in a bowl. Stir in lemon juice, oil, and parsley.

❧ BROAD BEAN: Serve cooked and peeled young fava beans with a soft-boiled egg over toast points.

❧ CÉLERI RÉMOULADE: Grate raw celery root and combine with lemon juice, mayonnaise, capers, and finely chopped pickles or gherkins. Let sit 30 minutes before serving.

❧ CHICKPEA SALAD: Cook until tender and combine with a vinaigrette heavily flavored with mustard. Stir in minced shallot and chopped fresh parsley or tarragon.

❧ CRUDITÉS WITH ANCHOVY SAUCE: Combine carrot and celery sticks, cauliflower and broccoli florets, and tiny green beans on a plate. Serve with *anchoïade* (page 188).

❧ CUCUMBER SALAD: Thinly slice and dress with vinaigrette enriched with yogurt or cream. Stir in chopped fresh mint and minced garlic. Serve chilled.

❧ EGGPLANT CAVIAR: Preheat the oven to 400°F. Halve an eggplant lengthwise and bake for 30 minutes or until soft, cut side up. Scrape out the soft, cooked pulp with a spoon. Mix the pulp with olive oil, salt, pepper, minced garlic, and chopped fresh herbs. Puree in a blender or food processor, or mash with the back of a spoon, to form a paste of spreadable consistency.

❧ ENDIVE AND GRUYÈRE SALAD: Slice Belgian endive and serve with small cubes of Gruyère cheese. Mix with a vinaigrette heavily flavored with mustard.

❧ GRATED VEGETABLE SALADS: Grate raw carrots, beets, black radish, parsnips, or turnips. Add chopped fresh herbs and finely chopped onion or shallot, and toss with vinaigrette.

❧ HERB AND SAUSAGE TERRINE: Steam 1 pound fresh spinach until wilted, then drain and chop. Place in a bowl and add ¼ cup chopped ham, 2 bacon slices chopped, 1 small onion finely chopped, 2 garlic cloves minced, and chopped mixed herbs (tarragon, parsley, savory, basil, etc.) to taste. Mix 1 pound of sausage meat with 2 lightly beaten eggs in a separate bowl and stir into the herb mixture. Season with salt and pepper and pour into an earthenware terrine. Set the terrine into a large pan of hot water and bake for about 1 hour in 350°F. oven. Let cool slightly, then place a small piece of wood or heavy cardboard over the surface. Place large cans on top to weight down the terrine and chill for at least 12 hours or overnight. Slice thinly before serving.

❧ LEEKS VINAIGRETTE: Select young, pencil-size leeks and steam until tender. While still hot, dry well and sprinkle with vinegar. Marinate a few hours in seasoned olive oil, then serve chilled.

❧ MACÉDOINE OF VEGETABLES: Combine cubes of cooked carrot, turnip, and potato in a bowl with sliced green beans, cooked green peas, and cooked baby lima beans. Bind with a lemon-based mayonnaise.

❧ MESCLUN SALAD: Combine arugula, mâche, curly endive, and radicchio in a large bowl. Toss with an olive-oil vinaigrette.

❧ MIXED GREENS AND ROQUEFORT: Crumble a small piece of Roquefort cheese into your favorite vinaigrette. Sprinkle with chopped fresh herbs and toss.

❧ MUSHROOMS OR ZUCCHINI À LA GRECQUE: Sauté sliced onions and either mushrooms or zucchini cubes in olive oil until softened, about 5 minutes. Add white wine, lemon juice, a touch of tomato paste, and coriander seeds and cook about 15 to 20 minutes more. Serve chilled.

❧ RED CABBAGE AND APPLE SALAD: Finely mince the cabbage and add slices of apple. Toss with a vinaigrette made with red wine vinegar.

❧ SALAD NIÇOISE: Layer sliced cooked potatoes, tiny green beans, hard-boiled egg, tomato, and tuna in a bowl. Toss with vinaigrette and garnish with anchovies and black olives. (Purists never use lettuce for this salad!)

❧ SALAD OF DANDELION AND OTHER WILD GREENS: Combine young and tender leaves with bits of fried bacon in a large bowl. Toss with vinaigrette made with red wine vinegar and heavily flavored with mustard.

❧ TOMATO AND CUCUMBER SALAD: Slice each and dress with a vinaigrette made with lime juice and chopped fresh mint.

❧ WATERCRESS OR ARUGULA SALAD WITH COOKED BEETS: Toss greens and beets with lemon juice and olive oil.

❧ VINAIGRETTE: Combine 1 tablespoon white wine vinegar or lemon juice, a pinch of salt and pepper, and 1 teaspoon prepared mustard in a small bowl. Blend well. Use a fork to beat in 3 tablespoons corn or olive oil. If desired, add additional flavorings such as a mashed anchovy fillet or fresh herbs. Makes enough to dress 2 cups of vegetables.

HOT DISHES FEATURING VEGETABLES

❧ ARTICHOKES BARIGOULE (PEASANT STYLE): Sauté tiny artichokes (about 1 inch long) in olive oil with a little bacon, onion, carrot, and tomato. Add white wine to cover and a bay leaf, chopped fresh parsley, and thyme and simmer until tender.

❧ BROAD BEANS (FAVA BEANS): Remove tough outer skins and steam until tender; reheat with savory in a little olive oil. Alternatively, stir cooked beans with the pan juices from a roast, sauté lightly in butter, or stir with some bacon bits.

❧ CAULIFLOWER: Brown fresh bread crumbs in butter until butter turns lightly nut-colored. Pour immediately over hot cooked cauliflower florets and serve at once.

❧ CUCUMBERS: Cook peeled and julienned cucumbers in butter over low heat until tender but not mushy, about 15 minutes. Sprinkle with salt, pepper, paprika, or chopped fresh herbs. A bit of leftover rice can be added if desired.

❧ FENNEL GRATIN: Preheat the oven to 400°F. Trim away the tough outer leaves of the fennel bulbs. Cut bulbs in half and steam until tender, about 10 minutes. Place in buttered baking dish, sprinkle with grated cheese, and dot with butter. Bake or broil until browned on top, about 5 minutes.

❧ LEEK OR ONION TART: Preheat the oven to 400°F. Line a tart pan with pie crust and set aside. Cook enough leek or onion slices in butter until soft but not brown to half-fill the mold. In a small bowl, beat together a couple of eggs and some milk or cream to fill the tarts. Season with salt, pepper, and freshly grated nutmeg. Pour over the leeks or onions and bake for about 45 minutes or until firm in the center and browned on top.

❧ ONIONS WITH STUFFING: Preheat the oven to 350°F. Parboil large onions for 10 minutes, then carefully remove the centers, leaving shells that measure about ¼ inch thick. Chop the centers and combine with ham, garlic, parsley, and a little bread that has been softened in milk. Stuff the onions with this mixture, sprinkle with grated cheese, and bake for about 50 minutes or until lightly browned on top.

❧ PATTYPAN SQUASH: Combine sliced pattypan squash with onions, bacon, parsley, and thyme. Cook slowly over medium heat, stirring often, until stewed, about 15 minutes.

❧ POTATO GRATIN (GRATIN DAUPHINOIS): Place a bay leaf in the bottom of a baking dish rubbed with garlic. Dot with butter and layer with thin potato slices. (Do not make the layer more than 1 inch deep.) Season with salt and pepper to taste, then pour in hot milk to almost cover. Dot with butter again and bake in a medium-hot oven about 30 minutes or until potatoes are tender and top is golden brown.

❧ RATATOUILLE: Cook cubes of onion, green pepper, eggplant, zucchini, and tomato with minced garlic, a bay leaf, and a sprig of fresh thyme over low heat in olive oil. Stew until softened, about 20 minutes, and season well with salt and pepper.

❧ RED CABBAGE AND APPLES: Layer thin slices of cabbage, apples, onions, and bacon in a heavy-bottomed pot. Add red wine and a bay leaf. Simmer until soft, about 1 hour. Serve with sausage.

🌿 SPINACH: Steam washed, stemmed leaves over low heat until wilted; the water that clings to the leaves after washing provides enough moisture. Add a squirt of lemon juice or stir in a little cream flavored with nutmeg, and serve.

🌿 SUMMER SQUASH: Preheat the oven to 350°F. Halve and spoon out the seeds and some flesh from yellow summer squash, zucchini, or pattypan squash to form a cavity. Fill each cavity with a stuffing made of chopped meat, onion, rice, and herbs. Place in a baking dish with bouillon or tomato sauce and bake until the squash is soft, about 40 minutes.

🌿 SWISS CHARD: Steam until tender, about 3 minutes. Pour off the fat from a pan in which beef or lamb has been roasted and add the steamed chard to the pan juices. Warm through and serve at once. Alternatively, add the steamed chard to either a plain cream sauce or a cream sauce seasoned with curry or mustard.

🌿 TOMATOES PROVENÇALES: Preheat the oven to 400°F. Cut firm but ripe tomatoes in half and sprinkle with chopped parsley, thyme, minced garlic, salt, pepper, and dried bread crumbs. Drizzle over a little olive oil and bake for about 10 minutes or until softened and lightly browned on top.

🌿 TURNIPS: Cook white turnips about 20 minutes or until tender and drain. Pour off the fat from a pan in which beef or lamb has been roasted and add the turnips to the pan juices. Warm through and serve at once. Alternatively, bake cooked turnips in a cheese sauce and serve very hot. Turnips make a good addition to a boiled beef dinner and are delicious in soups with potatoes and onions.

🌿 VEGETABLE FRITTERS: Slices of young eggplant, fennel, or zucchini—or comfrey leaves, or shiso (perilla) flowers—make good vegetable fritters. Coat with pancake batter, cook, and dry until crisp. Drain and serve.

🌿 VEGETABLE PUREES: Celery root, leeks, carrots, chestnuts, turnips, parsnips, Jerusalem artichokes (also known as sunchokes), squash, pumpkin, and onions all make good purees. Add cooked potatoes to the purees if desired.

🌿 ZUCCHINI: Sauté zucchini with sliced onions in olive oil or butter until softened, about 10 minutes. Stir in grated cheese and chopped fresh parsley just before serving.

🌿 CHICKEN BASQUAISE: Cut a medium chicken into serving pieces and brown in vegetable or olive oil. Remove to a plate or platter and add chopped onion, sliced red bell pepper, and sliced green bell pepper to pan. Cook, stirring often, until vegetables are softened, about 5 minutes. Stir in peeled tomatoes, crushed garlic, salt, and pepper to taste. Cook 5 minutes longer. Return the chicken to the pan, cover, and cook over medium-low heat until dark meat is no longer pink, about 20 minutes. About $\frac{1}{4}$ cup diced country ham can be added along with the tomatoes, if desired.

🌿 DAUBE PROVENÇALE: Place layers of diced salt pork, sliced onions, tomatoes, carrots, a bay leaf, thyme, parsley, and sliced stewing beef or lamb in a heavy pot rubbed with olive oil. Season well with salt and pepper. Top the meat with another layer of vegetables, and season again. Sprinkle minced garlic and orange peel over the top. Pour in red wine to almost cover, cover the pot, and simmer for 2 hours or until meat is tender. Chill, then remove fat that has solidified on the surface. Remove meat and vegetables, and strain liquid if desired. Return meat and vegetables to pot, add black olives, and simmer 10 minutes before serving.

❧ NAVARIN (SPRING LAMB STEW): Cook cubes of spring lamb in olive oil until lightly browned. Add a lot of minced garlic and a little flour and continue cooking until well browned. Pour in enough thin tomato sauce or hot water to cover and stir well. Add a bay leaf, bring to a simmer over medium heat, partially cover, reduce heat, and cook slowly for about 30 minutes. Add baby carrots, peeled young white turnips, small white onions, and new potatoes and simmer about 20 minutes. Add shelled peas or snow peas and cook 5 minutes longer. Sprinkle with chopped fresh parsley just before serving.

❧ POT AU FEU: Place meaty beef bones in a large soup pot or kettle. Add carrots, turnip, leeks, onions (1 stuck with a whole clove), bay leaf, and sprigs of fresh thyme and parsley. Pour in enough cold water to cover. Bring to a boil, then reduce heat to medium-low and simmer for 2 to 3 hours. Strain the broth, discard the solids, and return the broth to the pot. Bring to a boil, add a piece of stewing beef, and reduce the heat to medium-low. Gently simmer for 2 hours. Add the following prepared vegetables: carrots, whites of leeks, new potatoes, turnip, parley root, parsnips, and onions. Cook until the vegetables are soft but not mushy, 30 to 40 minutes. Traditionally served with coarse sea salt, mustards, pickles or chutney, toast, and poached beef marrow on the side.

(Note: Pot au Feu is sometimes served in two courses. The broth is served in bowls as the first course, then the meat and vegetables are eaten separately. Alternatively, the dish is served all at once in large plates or shallow bowls with the broth in the bottom.)

THE LESS COMMON VEGETABLES

❧ CARDOONS: Wrap stalks in straw and blanch in the garden for two weeks. Peel the cooking-ready stalks and cut into 2-inch-long pieces. Bring a large pot of water to a boil. Blend a few tablespoons of flour with the juice of half a lemon and add to the water. Drop the pieces into the water and cook until tender but not mushy, 30 to 40 minutes. Drain and combine with pan juices from a meat roast or bake in a white sauce until top is lightly browned.

❧ GREENS: Orach, amaranth, Malabar spinach, Good King Henry, or New Zealand spinach can be used as spinach in any recipe.

❧ CHERVIL ROOTS (PARSNIP CHERVIL): Peel and cut the roots into 1-inch-long pieces. Steam and serve with butter or cream. The roots can also be fried, sautéed, pureed, or baked in a white sauce. The vegetable can be served cold with hard-boiled eggs and a vinaigrette or mayonnaise.

❧ CHESTNUT SQUASH (POTIMARRON): Peel and remove seeds. This winter squash can be pureed or fried; used in a soufflé or tart; or the basis for beignets or croquettes. It can also be used in sweets such as cakes, ice cream, or jam.

❧ JERUSALEM ARTICHOKES (SUNCHOKES): Peel and grate, then serve raw in a salad with red cabbage, walnuts, and a vinaigrette made with yogurt and mustard. (Recipe courtesy of François Couplan, see p. 181.)

❧ PURSLANE: Serve raw in a salad. Add a little anchovy paste to a vinaigrette. Chill the purslane and toss with the sauce just before serving. (Recipe courtesy of François Couplan, see p. 181.)

❧ SALSIFY OR OYSTER PLANT: Peel and cut into 1-inch lengths. (Keep in acidulated water to prevent discoloration after peeling.) Add a small amount of flour to a large pot of water and bring to a boil. Cook the salsify until tender, about 10 minutes. Drain well and heat in melted butter for about 5 minutes. Sprinkle with chopped parsley just before serving.

❧ SEAKALE: Steam tender young shoots and serve with a vinaigrette or Hollandaise sauce, as for asparagus.

SAUCES

❧ AÏOLI: Add 2 finely minced garlic cloves per person to mayonnaise that has been made with olive oil.

❧ ANCHOÏADE: Crush 2 oil-packed anchovy fillets per person in a small bowl. Slowly beat in olive oil with a fork to make an emulsion. Add crushed garlic if desired.

❧ BURNET-YOGURT SAUCE: Mix finely chopped fresh burnet leaves with equal parts olive oil and yogurt. Season to taste with salt and pepper. (Recipe courtesy of François Couplan, see p. 181.)

❧ HERB SAUCE: Finely chop together a selection of fresh parsley, tarragon, chervil, and chives. Stir in lemon juice, salt, pepper, and a little olive oil or yogurt. Serve with fish or hard-boiled eggs. (Recipe courtesy of François Couplan, see p. 181.)

❧ SORREL SAUCE: Roughly chop 1 large handful of young sorrel leaves per person. Place in a saucepan and simmer, stirring often, over low heat until wilted. (There should be enough moisture that clings to the leaves to cook the sorrel.) Add crème fraîche to enrich, season with salt and pepper, and simmer for a few minutes. Continue cooking until the sauce reaches desired consistency. Traditionally served with fish.

❧ TOMATO COULIS: Cook 1 or 2 finely chopped onions in olive oil until softened, 3 to 5 minutes. Add chopped, peeled, and seeded tomatoes, thyme, and a bay leaf. Bring to a boil over high heat; reduce the heat to medium-high, and cook, stirring often, until thickened somewhat.

DESSERTS

❧ APRICOT MOUSSE: Push ½ pound of very ripe fresh apricots through a sieve to form a smooth puree. Fold in 1 cup sweetened whipped cream and chill well before serving.

❧ CHERRY CLAFOUTIS: Preheat the oven to 350°F. Blend together 3 eggs, ½ cup sugar, and ½ cup flour. Beat in 2 cups milk and a pinch of salt. Butter a 1-quart gratin dish and arrange 1 pound of pitted cherries over the bottom. Pour or spoon in the egg mixture, then bake in upper part of oven for about 40 minutes or until risen and golden.

❧ FRUIT SORBET: Boil 1½ cups water and ¾ cup sugar over medium-low heat until the sugar dissolves and the syrup is slightly thickened, about 5 minutes. Cool completely. Stir in 2 cups fruit pulp and 1 tablespoon lemon juice. Freeze in an ice cream maker according to manufacturer's instructions.

🍃 FRUIT TART: Preheat the oven to 400°F. Line a 9-inch tart mold with sweet tart pastry. Brush the interior with beaten egg white (especially important if the fruit is very juicy). Sprinkle with sugar and decoratively arrange slices of fruit—use apples, pears, plums, apricots or peaches, for example—on the bottom of the mold. Sprinkle the fruit with lemon juice and sugar to taste (fruit will become more tart as it cooks) and bake in the upper part of oven for about 30 minutes or until the pastry is golden. Serve with custard sauce, ice cream, or crème fraîche.

For variations, (1) use less sugar and drizzle honey over the tart just after removing it from the oven; (2) spread a layer of thick applesauce on the pastry before arranging the fruit if making an apple tart; (3) beat 2 eggs and ½ cup milk or cream with sugar and vanilla and spoon over the fruit before baking for an Alsatian-style tart; or (4) sprinkle slivers of almonds over the fruit before baking when making a pear tart.

🍃 HERBAL ICE CREAM: Use mint, lavender, thyme, rosemary, lemon verbena, or other aromatic herb. Scald 2 cups milk with the herb of choice. Cool and infuse, then remove the herb. Beat 3 egg yolks together with 4 tablespoons sugar and a pinch of salt in a heatproof bowl. Gently reheat the milk and pour over the yolks. Pour the contents of the bowl back into the pan and cook over low heat, stirring often, until the mixture forms a custard that just coats the back of a wooden spoon. Chill, then freeze in an ice cream maker according to manufacturer's instructions.

🍃 PEAR COMPOTE: Poach ripe but firm pears in red wine with prunes and sugar. Alternatively, poach pears in red wine with a whole clove and a cinnamon stick, or in black currant jam (or syrup) thinned with water. Remove the pears to a serving dish when cooked, then reduce the cooking liquid over high heat until thickened. Add *crème de cassis* (black currant liqueur) to pears poached in jam and spoon over the pears. Chill before serving.

🍃 PEACH MELBA: Peel ripe peaches, halve, and remove the pits. Poach in a light sugar syrup until tender, then chill. Serve with vanilla ice cream and pureed raspberries. (Do not cook the peaches if they are very ripe.)

🍃 QUINCE COMPOTE: Peel, quarter, and remove the seeds from quince and rub surfaces with lemon juice. Place in a large saucepan and cover with water. Add sugar to taste and a vanilla bean. Simmer over medium heat until the fruit is soft, about 30 minutes. Remove the quince to a serving bowl and discard the vanilla bean. Reduce the cooking juices over high heat until thick and syrupy. Pour over the fruit and chill.

🍃 STRAWBERRIES IN RED WINE: Place hulled and sliced strawberries in a serving dish and sprinkle with sugar. Pour in enough red wine to barely cover. Chill for at least 1 hour before serving.

OTHER FRUIT AND HERB PREPARATIONS

🍃 BLACK CURRANT LIQUEUR: Use 1 quart of 80-proof alcohol per 2 pounds of fresh berries. Wash the fruit and dry well. Place in a glass or earthenware jug along with a few currant leaves. Cover with alcohol, place lid on top, and let sit in a dark place for about

2 months. Strain and reserve the alcohol. Heat 2 cups water with 2½ cups sugar until boiling. Add this syrup to the alcohol and pour into sterilized jars. Seal and store in dark place until ready to serve.

❧ FLOWER AND HERB JELLY: Coarsely chop 1 pound unpeeled apples and place in a large saucepan. Reserve the seeds tied securely in a small piece of cheesecloth. Cover with 2 quarts water and bring to a boil over high heat. Reduce the heat to medium-low, add the apple seed packet, and simmer until the apples are soft, about 5 minutes. Strain through a sieve without pressing. Add 8 cups sugar and the juice of 1 lemon per quart of juice. Bring to a boil and cook, stirring, until reduced and jellied. Add 2 quarts of edible flower petals or leaves (rose petals, violets, orange flowers, or mint leaves, for example). Bring back to a boil and pour into sterilized jars and seal.

❧ HERB WINE: Place 3 sprigs of your favorite herb (bee balm, tarragon, woodruff, or hyssop, for example) in a bottle of good white wine. Leave in a cool spot for 48 hours to macerate. Filter the wine and serve as an apéritif.

❧ INFUSIONS OR HERB TEAS: Select your favorite herb or blend of herbs (lemon verbena, thyme, sage, rosemary, or mint, for example) and put 2 sprigs in a teapot. Pour over just barely boiled water and let sit about 5 minutes before pouring (the herb can be removed at this time if desired).

❧ PICKLED CHERRY TOMATOES: Choose firm ripe or still-green tomatoes. Carefully prick each tomato 2 or 3 times with a needle. Place in preserving jars and layer with thyme sprigs, bay leaves, tarragon leaves (or other fresh herbs), salt, and peppercorns. Fill the jars with white vinegar and 2 whole cloves per jar, cover tightly, and store for 2 to 3 months before using.

❧ BACHELOR'S JAM (PRESERVED FRUIT): In a large glass jar, make layers of summer fruit as the season progresses. Place strawberries, peaches, plums (whatever is on hand) in the bottom of the jar and layer with sugar. Cover with a good-quality clear brandy like kirsch. When full, seal and store in a dark place for at least six months, then serve in small dessert glasses or over ice cream.

❧ QUINCE JAM: Gently clean the quinces with a clean towel. Cut the fruit into quarters but do not peel. Place in a saucepan and pour in cold water to cover. Cook over medium heat until barely cooked, about 20 minutes. Strain. Peel and cut the pulp into slices or cubes. Add to the juice and weigh the mixture. Add 2 cups sugar for every quart of juice and pulp. If desired, add 1 or 2 vanilla beans. Boil gently until reduced, thickened, and deep red. Remove vanilla beans, if used. Pour into sterilized jars and seal.

RECIPE
SUGGESTIONS

INDEX

RECIPE INDEX

Designed by Joel Avirom

Design Assistant: Jason Snyder
Design Production: Meghan Day Healey

Typefaces in this book are
Spectrum, designed by Jan van Krimpen
and Poliphilus, based on designs by
Francesco Griffo

Printed by Grafiche Milani
in Milan, Italy